Mission for Mother

Mission for Mother

Guiding the Child

by

G. Hugh Allred

BOOKCRAFT
Salt Lake City, Utah
1968

6th Printing, 1972

Cynthia 73
Patrick 74

LITHOGRAPHED IN U.S.A. BY

PUBLISHERS PRESS
SALT LAKE CITY, UTAH

Dedication

Affectionately dedicated to Carolyn, my wife, whose valuable assistance made this book possible, and to my children, Steven, Lynnette and Sharlene.

Preface

Mission for Mother is written for the purpose of assisting mothers in the challenging task of training and disciplining their children. Effective motherhood is basic to the well-being of the child and society for it is Mother who usually has the greatest influence on her child's becoming a happy and constructive adult citizen. There are many forces at work in today's world undermining Mother's ability to train her children effectively. It is the author's objective to provide guidelines which will help mothers to become more assured, happy and competent in a most demanding profession.

The ideal is for Mother and Father to function as a cooperative team in rearing children. In reality, however, Mother is alone with her young children much of the time and must then rely on her own resources to train and discipline them. Possibly because of this and the close, intensive relationship Mother experiences with her young children, the author has found that it is she who is usually most troubled by her children, not Father. For these reasons, the author has written this book for Mother. If Father wants assistance, he will find value in reading *Mission for Mother* for the principles also apply to him.

The author is greatly indebted to Dr. Alfred Adler and Dr. Rudolf Dreikurs for their knowledge, understanding and great insight regarding the family. Much of this book is based on their writings. The author is also deeply indebted to his association with Dr. Oscar C. Christensen and Dr. Raymond Lowe of the Community Parent-Teacher Education Center at the University of Oregon in Eugene, Oregon. It was in this family counseling center the author spent two years digesting the ideas, theories and counseling practices of these fine gentlemen. The approach of this book is based primarily on the writings and teachings of these four men, for the author believes their approach is effective and closely allied to basic Christian principles.

Special appreciation is extended to Richard Allen, Assistant Professor of Languages at Brigham Young University, who so willingly gave of his time to edit the manuscript. The author is also grateful to Dr. Eugene Mead, Assistant Professor of Child Development and Family Relations at Brigham Young University, and to Brother Reed Morrill, Brigham Young University Counselor, for their helpful suggestions.

Contents

I. The Objectives 1

II. A Psychological Foundation 18

III. The Religious Foundation 32

IV. Principles for Attaining the Objectives 45

V. Applying the Principles 74

VI. Correcting the Misbehavior 116

VII. Some Do's and Don'ts — A Review 240

VIII. Getting Started 249

Introduction

Mother provides the protective environment wherein the fertilized cell grows and develops until it becomes a fully developed baby that finds birth into the world of mortal experiences. It is she who gives the child his first emotional relationship experiences, which become the model for his later relationships with his fellowman. Mother is instrumental in starting the child on the path toward eternal, God-like life.

President David O. McKay referred to motherhood as the greatest of all the vocations and the most beautiful of all the arts. If one were to search for the most outstanding calling in life, he suggested motherhood as the standard against which it should be measured. He has said that motherhood is the most powerful influence among men, the noblest of the professions.

Being a successful mother requires a great amount of energy, knowledgeably and intelligently applied to the art of rearing children. Probably Mother's first step for improving her child-rearing practices is that of forming a clear concept of and making explicit those qualities and traits of character she wants her child to develop. The purpose of Chapter I is to help Mother clarify these objectives by presenting for her consideration positive character traits that are worthy of the child. An attempt has been made to combine references from Holy Writ and from literature of psychology in order to set forth objectives that are psychologically, socially, and religiously sound.

The Objectives

Objective One — Love for God

> Thou shalt love the Lord thy God with all thy heart, and with all thy soul, and with all thy mind.
>
> This is the first and great commandment. (Matt. 22:37-38)

The devout mother will want to rear children who have a deep and abiding reverence for God. The objective should be that of rearing children who desire to communicate prayerfully with their Heavenly Father at a very personal level. They should experience the feeling that they have God's approval and are truly His sons and daughters. She will desire that her children love God and show this love by keeping His commandments.

> If a man love me, he will keep my words: and my Father will love him, and we will come unto him, and make our abode with him. (John 14:23)

Objective Two — Self-Respect and Self-Acceptance

Mother's objectives should include rearing children who accept and respect themselves as being children of our Heavenly Father. There are many who do not. One of the reasons for this seems to be the tendency to equate humility with self-abasement. This is a pernicious interpretation of the doctrine of humility. Our Heavenly Father wants us to like and respect ourselves.

> Jesus said unto him . . . Thou shalt *love* thy neighbour as *thyself*. (Matt. 22:37-39)

Another problem which interferes with a person's thinking well of himself is a misunderstanding of Church and Gospel principles associated with man's relationship to his fellow man. We read in Matthew, Chapter 5, verses 38-41 the following:

> Ye have heard that it has been said, An eye for an eye and a tooth for a tooth:
>
> But I say unto you, That ye resist not evil: but whosoever shall smite thee on thy right cheek, turn to him the other also
>
> And if any man will sue thee at the law, and take away thy coat, let him have thy cloke also.
>
> And whosoever shall compel thee to go a mile, go with him twain.

Many mistakenly interpret this to mean that the devout should always submit to the demands of their fellowmen. This interpretation creates serious problems for them and for those with whom they interact. They tend to become victims of others who would control them by making their decisions and telling them what to do. By giving up their lives to the manipulations of others, they soon dislike themselves. An individual who always "turns the other cheek" soon betrays his own values and eventually loses his identity as he submerges himself beneath the wishes and demands of powerful associates.

Jesus (whom we are to use as our example) did not submit to others indiscriminately. This is evident in the following references:

> Then Peter took him, and began to rebuke him, saying, Be it far from thee, Lord: this shall not be unto thee.
>
> But he turned, and said unto Peter, *Get thee behind me, Satan:* thou art an offence unto me: for thou savourest not the things that be of God, but those that be of men. (Matt. 16:22-23)
>
> Again, the devil taketh him up into an exceeding high mountain, and sheweth him all the kingdoms of the world, and the glory of them;
>
> And saith unto him, All these things will I give thee, if thou wilt fall down and worship me.
>
> Then saith Jesus unto him, Get thee hence, Satan: for it is written, Thou shalt worship the Lord thy God, and him only shalt thou serve. (Matt. 4:8-10)
>
> And the Jews' passover was at hand, and Jesus went up to Jerusalem,
>
> And found in the temple those that sold oxen and sheep and doves, and the changers of money sitting:

And when he had made a scourge of small cords, he drove them all out of the temple, and the sheep, and the oxen; and poured out the changers' money, and overthrew the tables;

And said unto them that sold doves, Take these things hence; make not my Father's house an house of merchandise. (John 2:13-16)

Matthew also tells of Christ driving money changers from the temple of God:

And Jesus went into the temple of God, and cast out all them that sold and bought in the temple, and overthrew the tables of the moneychangers, and the seats of them that sold doves,

And said unto them, It is written, My house shall be called the house of prayer; but ye have made it a den of thieves. (Matt. 21:12-13)

Christ could, at times, be very harsh with those whom he considered deserving of rebuke.

Then spake Jesus to the multitude, and to his disciples,

Saying, The scribes and the Pharisees sit in Moses' seat:

All therefore whatsoever they bid you observe, that observe and do; but do not ye after their works: for they say, and do not.

For they bind heavy burdens and grievous to be borne, and lay them on men's shoulders; but they themselves will not move them with one of their fingers.

But all their works they do for to be seen of men: they make broad their phylacteries, and enlarge the borders of their garments . . .

But woe unto you, scribes and Pharisees, hypocrites! for ye shut up the kingdom of heaven against men: for ye neither go in yourselves, neither suffer ye them that are entering to go in.

Woe unto you, scribes and Pharisees, hypocrites! for ye devour widows' houses, and for a pretence make long prayer: therefore ye shall receive the greater damnation.

Woe unto you, scribes and Pharisees, hypocrites! for ye compass sea and land to make one proselyte, and when he is made, ye make him twofold more the child of hell than yourselves.

Woe unto you, ye blind guides, which say, Whosoever shall swear by the temple, it is nothing; but whosoever shall swear by the gold of the temple, he is a debtor!

Ye fools and blind: for whether is greater, the gold, or the temple that sanctifieth the gold? . . .

Ye blind guides, which strain at a gnat, and swallow a camel . . .

Even so ye also outwardly appear righteous unto men, but within ye are full of hypocrisy and iniquity.

Woe unto you, scribes and Pharisees, hypocrites! because ye build the tombs of the prophets, and garnish the sepulchres of the righteous . . .

Ye serpents, ye generation of vipers, how can ye escape the damnation of hell? (Matt. 23:1-5, 13-17, 24, 28-29, 33)

For a faithful Christian turning the other cheek does not mean to become another man's puppet, nor to compromise one's principles. It simply means to refuse to play the other's "dirty game," to disengage from disrespectful relationships.

Also, by not communicating to others — "Hey, step back, you're stepping on my toe" — we withhold corrective feedback that could be used by them in learning more respect for other people.

If our children truly love themselves, they will not be unnecessarily burdened by artificial guilt, crippling shame, or anxiety. They will enjoy eating, sleeping, and the sexual experiences of marriage. They will enjoy having a body which our Heavenly Father has given them and will be free from disgust and aversion concerning it, its products, odors, and functions. If we train our children to like themselves, they will tend to live happy lives.

Objective Three — Compassion for the Whole of Mankind

Man has forgotten how to love his fellowman. To rear children who, as adults, have a warm, loving and respectful feeling toward mankind in general, is a most worthy objective. We look all about us and find family members, neighborhoods, states and nations quarreling and fighting. In the political, social and sometimes religious areas of life, there seems to be strife. Man too often relates to his fellow-man in a vertical, superior-inferior fashion. This results in an emphasis on getting ahead of others. Stepping on others as one climbs rapidly up the ladder of economic, social, or religious success is often viewed as the only method. As long as man emphasizes superiority and inferiority rather than equality, a lack of love will persist.

The way children learn to treat one another in the family tends to be the way they will treat others. Parents are, therefore, in a very influential position. This is especially true of Mother. It is hoped that one of her objectives is to rear children who, as adults, have a kindly feeling towards others. They identify and empathize with the whole of mankind. They have a genuine desire to help others and to regard all persons as members of a large, single family. They have a genuine affection for their brothers, even though they be foolish, weak, or obnoxious at times. Our children should have developed, by the time they are adults, a genuine underlying feeling of kinship with others, regardless of their class, political belief, education, color or race. They should respect those who are competent in their own trades or skills regardless of whether such people work primarily with their hands or brains.

The child should develop into a democratic individual whose judgements of others would be based on such things as traits of character, rather than name, family, race, age, and power or fame.

Our children, as they grow up, should be capable of developing deep interpersonal relationships with a few people and have friendly ties with most. They should be capable of loving profoundly. Such things as benevolence, affection and friendliness for all, patience for the weaknesses in others, and a tender love for children are desired qualities.

As our children develop a oneness with humanity, they should have the ability to see clearly the hypocritical, pretentious, and pompous, and, on occasion, appropriately confront those who deserve it. The confrontation should be done with genuine love, it should be deserved and of benefit to those confronted.

A feeling of oneness with mankind is suggested in Luke, Chapter 6, verses 32-35, when Christ said the following:

> For if ye love them which love you, what thank have ye? for sinners also love those that love them.
>
> And if ye do good to them which do good to you, what thank have ye? for sinners also do even the same.
>
> And if ye lend to them of whom ye hope to receive, what thank have ye? for sinners also lend to sinners, to receive as much again.
>
> But love ye your enemies, and do good, and lend, hoping for nothing again; and your reward shall be great, and ye shall be the children of the Highest: for he is kind unto the unthankful and to the evil.

In John we read:

> Beloved, let us love one another: for love is of God; and every one that loveth is born of God, and knoweth God.
>
> He that loveth not knoweth not God; for God is love. (I John 4:7-8)
>
> For *all the law is fulfilled* in one word, even in this; Thou shalt *love thy neighbour* as thyself. (Gal. 5:14)
>
> By this shall all men know that ye are my disciples, if ye have love one to another. (John 13:35)

One of the most thought-provoking revelations concerning how man should feel and relate towards his fellowman is found in the Doctrine and Covenants, section 121, verses 41-44.

> No power or influence can or ought to be maintained by virtue of the priesthood, only by persuasion, by long-suffering, by gentleness and meekness, and by love unfeigned;
>
> By kindness, and pure knowledge, which shall greatly enlarge the soul without hypocrisy, and without guile —

Reproving betimes with sharpness, when moved upon by
the Holy Ghost; and then showing forth afterwards an increase
of love toward him whom thou hast reproved, lest he esteem
thee to be his enemy;

That he may know that thy faithfulness is stronger than
the cords of death.

One of the most beautiful guidelines is given in 2 Nephi, chapter 26, verse 33.

For none of these iniquities come of the Lord; for he doeth
that which is good among the children of men; and he doeth
nothing save it be plain unto the children of men; and he
inviteth them all to come unto him and partake of his goodness;
and he denieth none that come unto him, black and white, bond
and free, male and female; and he remembereth the heathen;
and all are alike unto God, both Jew and Gentile.

If God views all men equally, is it any wonder that man
should have compassion for his brothers?

Paul in the first epistle to the Corinthians as found in
Chapter 13, verses 1-13, indicates the importance of compassion:

Though I speak with the tongues of men and of angels,
and have not charity, I am become as sounding brass, or a
tinkling cymbal.

And though I have the gift of prophecy, and understand
all mysteries, and all knowledge; and though I have all faith,
so that I could remove mountains, and have not charity, I am
nothing.

And though I bestow all my goods to feed the poor, and
though I give my body to be burned, and have not charity,
it profiteth me nothing.

Charity suffereth long, and is kind; charity envieth not;
charity vaunteth not itself, is not puffed up . . .

Charity never faileth: but whether there be prophecies,
they shall fail; whether there be tongues, they shall cease; whether
there be knowledge, it shall vanish away . . .

And now abideth faith, hope, charity, these three; but the
greatest of these is charity.

And Paul, writing to the Romans, communicated the following:

> . . . and *if there be any other commandment*, it is briefly comprehended in this saying, namely, *Thou shalt love thy neighbour* as thyself.
>
> Love worketh no ill to his neighbour: therefore love is the fulfilling of the law. (Romans 13:9-10)

The basic need in today's world is for men to truly love one another. If men loved one another, there would be no wars, nor wealth and poverty existing side by side, nor would one man be inferior to another because of name, race or nationality. Mother is in a strategic position for how she trains her children will greatly determine whether or not they learn to relate to their fellowman in a spirit of cooperation and in an atmosphere of respect and love.

Objective Four — Honesty

Possibly one of the great needs for the well-being of the individual and society is honesty. To become civilized has too often meant to put on a facade, to play the game and say to people what it is thought would be pleasing to them. Many interpersonal relationships have become a sham of hidden, subtle cues that mean one thing and of verbalized words that say another. Dishonest interpersonal relationships create conflict and personal, emotional difficulties.

Our children, when they attain adulthood, should be honest in their dealings with all, including their children, spouses and professional, business, and religious acquaintances. Mother should train her children in such a manner that they are honest regardless of the setting or time. Sincerity, truthfulness, and integrity are hallmarks of the authentic, healthy individual.

In group counseling and therapy, one of the prime objectives is to train people to deal openly and honestly with one another. Change in behavior is encouraged through honest feedback from others. Most emotional illness involves dishonesty in interpersonal relationships.

There are many forces, especially in the mass communication media, that encourage dishonesty subtly and openly. It is imperative that people learn to interact honestly one with another if they are to achieve a high degree of happiness.

Objective Five — Reality

It is usually most difficult for those experiencing emotional difficulty to see their world as it really exists. Many tend to perceive what they wish rather than what is real. Ignoring reality gets them into serious difficulties. An example of this are clients who come to psychologists with deep feelings of anxiety and fear, but talk about their world and all their interpersonal relationships being beautiful. They may be having serious problems with their spouse, parents, or someone else very close to them — and deny the existence of any difficulty. This the Lord never intended, for he wants us to cope with reality effectively; this requires accurate, realistic perception.

Not only should Mother train her child to see the good and lovely in the world, but she should also train him to be consciously aware of the evil, regardless of how nasty or threatening it may be.

One of the obstacles that may get in Mother's way is an erroneous opinion suggesting that we should never judge our fellowmen. Some even go so far as to suggest that the faults in other people should not be seen. Those who develop the ability of *not* seeing the evil manipulations of others soon become their victims. They tend to overlook evil and pretend it does not exist. Actually, this is the coward's way out because by not seeing problems one does not have to deal with them. Soon the perceptions of the person who first works at not seeing clearly become dulled until he is no longer able to perceive accurately. This is also a disservice to others because by not perceiving accurately he is not able to give others corrective feedback that might help them to be better individuals.

Man must see realistically and accurately if he is to cope effectively with this mixed-up world and thereby return into the presence of his Heavenly Father. Mother's duty is to teach her child to recognize the furies, the evils in the world, and courageously respond to them.

The mother who teaches her children accurately will help them to see that there is usually bad mixed in with the good and some good mixed in with even the very bad. They will be able to perceive that even a man like Hitler was not completely bad and that some of our greatest prophets have had their problems. Such men as Joseph Smith, Peter, and John the Beloved were not completely good all the time. When the child learns to perceive people accurately, he will see that even the best are not perfect; this will make him more tolerant of himself and will give him the courage to keep trying in spite of his mistakes. He will not demand immediate perfection of himself now and, therefore, will have the courage and the strength to make mistakes and continue to grow and develop.

In summary, it is suggested that Mother be concerned about training her child to perceive accurately and honestly regardless of the threat so that he can more effectively cope with life's problems and, thereby, be able to enter back into the presence of his Heavenly Father.

Objective Six — Courage to Progress Continually

A frequent problem facing counselors and psychologists are those individuals who have become so discouraged that they are no longer trying to improve themselves. They have labeled themselves failures and believe they cannot succeed in improving themselves. Often the desire for immediate perfection discourages the child to such an extent that he gives up. When the demands and expectations of parents are too great, the child loses his courage to progress. The reverse is also true, for children become discouraged when parents set standards and expectations which are too low. Children in such circumstances adopt the feeling that, "If no one cares enough about me, then I do not care about myself," and they give up trying. Mother should take care to set standards which the child feels within himself are desirable and reachable. This will help him to have the stamina and resilience necessary to keep striving in the face of difficulties.

It is sometimes only through striving alone by trial and error that progress can take place. Because of this, man was sent on earth to live apart from his Heavenly Father to learn through pain, toil, and struggle to develop his own character. As he toils, he will make mistakes. When this occurs, he should have the courage to repent, which is a prerequisite to progress. Patriarch Eldred G. Smith has ably expressed this in an article, "The Need for Repentance," which appeared in the *Improvement Era,* November, 1949, page 718.

> As a steel which is heated and quenched becometh much stronger and more valuable, as a result of that tempering, so do we become stronger and more valuable as we overcome our sins, be they great or small. Each one has his trials to go through, and they all seem to be different. In the process of this tempering of the soul of man, we learn one great principle among many others: The need for repentance. It is this spirit of repentance the Lord requests as prerequisite to baptism, that through the act of repentance, man may start on the road to perfection and receive baptism and the Holy Ghost. But repentance does not stop there. That is the beginning of progress; and *as soon as repentance stops, progress stops.*

The following scriptures indicate the importance of repentance.

> Either what woman having ten pieces of silver, if she lose one piece, doth not light a candle, and sweep the house, and seek diligently till she find it?
>
> And when she hath found it, she calleth her friends and her neighbours together, saying, Rejoice with me; for I have found the piece which I had lost.

Likewise, I say unto you, there is joy in the presence of the angels of God over one sinner that repenteth. (Luke 15:8-10)

Yea, I would that ye would come forth and harden not your hearts any longer; for behold, now is the time and the day of your salvation; and therefore, if ye will repent and harden not your hearts, immediately shall the great plan of redemption be brought about unto you. (Alma 34:31)

For, behold, the Lord your Redeemer suffered death in the flesh; wherefore he suffered the pain of all men, that all men might repent and come unto him.

. . . on conditions of repentance. (D&C 18:11-12)

The Lord is not slack concerning his promise, as some men count slackness; but is longsuffering to us-ward, not willing that any should perish, but that all should come to repentance. (II Peter 3:9)

It is hoped that mothers of Israel train their children so they have the stamina and resilience to always work at improving their behavior through the principle of repentance. This suggests courage to commit themselves to a life of continued striving for self growth and mastery.

Objective Seven — Self-Reliance

A desirable objective is to rear children who become peaceful, serene adults. One of the best ways of achieving this is to train children to become self-reliant. They will then tend to become adults who are relatively independent of the artificial demands of their culture and of others. Our children should learn to base their thoughts and actions on principle, not people. Those who base their thinking and behavior on the desires and whims of others find that life is indeed stormy and unpredictable. Those who base their lives on principle find a relative constancy and freedom.

People who have learned self-reliance are indeed beautiful to behold. They have faith and trust in themselves, think well of themselves, walk with their shoulders back and their heads erect and they feel good toward others, their Heavenly Father, and life in general. Self-reliant people are relatively stable and serene as they experience hard knocks, deprivation, and frustrations. They are unmoved by the flattery of others. They do not search for reward, prestige, status, honors and love of others at any price. They continue to grow and develop apart from the artificiality and encumbrances of their society and culture.

These people are conventional and conforming in those things which are unimportant such as clothes, food, and language: however, they are able to be unconventional and unconforming when it is important that they fight against the errors of individuals, groups, or the masses. They may even feel somewhat detached from the general culture about them for they adopt it selectively. It is somewhat like being in the world, but not a part of it. These people are ruled by laws that they have accepted. They base their behavior on principle, not the whims or pressures of others.

Self-reliant people tend to interact with their culture or environment in rather complex ways. They are fluid in things that do not matter, but firm in those things which are of real importance. Mothers who rear their children to think well of themselves, to have the courage to fight for their rights and what they consider to be right, regardless of the odds, and to base their behavior and thoughts on principle rather than on the pressures of individuals or groups of people, will stimulate them to serenity and happiness. Some of the most tragic, emotional cripples are those who have given up their lives to the manipulations of others.

Objective Eight — Efficiency in Solving Problems

Another worthy objective is that of training children to meet life's difficulties and problems in a "problem-centered" manner. What is meant by "problem-centered" is the ability to successfully attack a problem with a minimum of effort. Many people in our family, Church, and business meetings expend vast amounts of time and energy in maneuvers having to do with inter-personal relationships that are not related to the problem or task at hand. And even when the problems have to do with interpersonal relationships, the activities are often not for the purpose of resolving the difficulties as much as they are revenge and ego-centered. Children should be reared so that when they approach life's tasks, they are relatively free of personal or selfish motives that interfere with efficient problem solving."

"Problem-centered" people work in a framework of broad, basic values rather than petty, local values which have no bearing on the problems of an eternal nature. It is hoped our children learn to be above the small things and have a wide breadth of vision which will enable them as adults to cope more realistically with problems confronting them. Mothers should train their children to see life in its broad total context. Pettiness, narrowness, and selfishness should have little part in the lives of those who are problem-centered.

Objective Nine — Openness

Being open to life is one of the most difficult challenges facing many in our society. The quality of keeping child-like openness, which is so valuable in living a Christ-like life, is probably lost to most adults. Children have a freshness of appreciation, a spontaneity, a creativeness about them which they too often lose as a result of the way adults respond to them in the home and school. These God-given gifts, which are so freely bestowed on the young, are crippled by adults who ignorantly respond in ways which inhibit and stunt their growth.

Mothers can encourage their children to openness by being keenly aware and appreciative of nature, others, and themselves. They can become sensitive to the basic good things of life and view these with pleasure, wonder, awe, and at times, even ecstacy. A deep appreciation for the beautiful and lovely in life makes life worth living.

Mothers can train their children to be more sensitive to the beauties of life by encouraging them to view nature in detail. This could include such things as a beautiful sunset, a wood lot, a puppy, and even their own body. There is no reason for our children to turn to drugs as adolescents and adults to increase their sensitiveness to life.

A part of openness is spontaneity. Because children tend to be natural, simple, and spontaneous, much of their behavior is beautiful. This spontaneity should be encouraged and increased rather than hindered. There is nothing more beautiful than an adult who is free and spontaneous in body movements, speech, and thought. They see things realistically and respond spontaneously.

People who are open also tend to be creative. They are original and inventive. There is a freshness and efficiency of perception which is a concomitant of openness. They tend to see the real and true more easily and spontaneously and, therefore, are more naturally effective in their responses. Children who are encouraged by their mothers to remain open tend to be more honest, sincere, and perceptive, as well as more creative. They tend to be beautiful children and to grow into beautiful adults.

Objective Ten — Moderation in All Things

One of the secrets to successful living is that of establishing a balance in all that is done. It is difficult for many to find this middle way. A mother who is truly interested in her child's happiness will train her child to be sensitive to the balanced life.

Too much of even the good in life becomes a sin rather than a benefit. Play can be detrimental or heathful for man. Over concern for the temporal things of life can also be detrimental. It is found, for example, that many people who spend all of their time with the temporal things of this world are, in reality, escaping from spiritual responsibilities. It is also often found that those who spend all of their time in spiritual endeavors are escaping from such temporal responsibilities as the economic, social training and discipline needs of family members. The principle of balance can be applied to almost every phase of living.

This is true of eating, sleeping, sexual, economic, social, and recreational activities. The objective of Mother is to rear children who are sensitive to a balanced life, a life of moderation.

Summary

In summary, it is suggested that Mother establish explicitly her objectives for training and disciplining her children. It is proposed that she rear children whose qualities as adults include the following:

1. A deep, reverential feeling and love for God.

2. An acceptance and respect for the self, both as it is and as it can become.

3. A feeling of respect, kinship, and compassion for mankind.

4. Honesty in their dealings with their fellowmen and themselves.

5. The courage and ability to see life realistically, the evil as well as the good.

6. The courage and strength for continued growth through a commitment to the principle of repentance.

7. Self-reliance and the ability to be relatively independent of their fellowmen, having lives based on principles, not people.

8. A concern with the relevant problems of life rather than inconsequential tasks that dissipate energy and result in little being accomplished.

9. Openness, which enables them to appreciate nature, people, and the meaningful experiences which they have.

10. Sensitivity to a balance in all things and the ability to moderate their lives in such a manner that they can effectively accomplish those tasks that are necessary for successful living.

These are some of the broad, general objectives that Mother may consider as she works at training her children so that they can enter back into the presence of their Heavenly Father. Chapter II is concerned with psychological considerations that serve as a foundation from which techniques and methods are built for rearing children; Chapter III will discuss the religious basis.

REFERENCES

Bennion, Adam S. *What It Means to be a Mormon.* Salt Lake City: The Deseret Sunday School Union, Publishers, 1917.

Berrett, William E. *Teachings of the Book of Mormon.* Salt Lake City: Deseret News Press, 1952.

The Holy Bible.

Jordan, E. *The Good Life.* Chicago: The University of Chicago Press, 1949.

Maslow, A. H. *Motivation and Personality.* New York: Harper and Row, Publishers, 1954.

Sicher, Lydia. "Education for Freedom," *The American Journal of Individual Psychology,* Vol. XI, No. 2, 1955.

The Book of Mormon. Salt Lake City: The Church of Jesus Christ of Latter-day Saints, Publishers.

Tanner, Obert C. *Christ's Ideals for Living.* Salt Lake City: The Deseret Sunday School Union Board, Publishers, 1955.

CHAPTER II.

A Psychological Foundation

Behavior Is Purposeful

A child's behavior is purposeful. In order for Mother to understand her child she must understand what purpose or goal the child is striving for whenever he misbehaves. Misbehavior cannot be effectively dealt with unless the one who is attempting to correct it understands the child's goal. Goals are the basic, psychic stimulation motivating an individual's behavior. The life of man is largely determined by the goals that he sets for himself. His goals of the future are much more important than his past history.

The child is usually *not consciously aware of his goals*. Though they are his own creation, they are only dimly seen by him. This is especially true when referring to those goals he repeatedly sets for himself.

Some of the goals a child elects to pursue may have rather neurotic qualities and be based on mistaken assumptions that he has about life; however, they seem logical to him and support his established perceptions.

The Basic Driving Force

The child's basic striving is to belong, to find a secure place with the significant people in his life. Such striving is considered a primary motivation of the child, not secondary.

Some suggest that the basic cause of anxiety is the fear of not belonging, of being isolated in a world of people who are hostile or non-accepting. Hall and Lindzy reported Horney as suggesting that we tend to react in three general ways. We move either towards people, away from them, or against them. Glasser suggested that the two basic needs of all are the needs to love and be loved, and the need to feel that we are worthwhile to ourselves and others. He proposed that we all have the same needs, but we vary in our ability to fulfill them. For Glasser, all people who come for psychiatric help are lacking in their ability to fulfill these love needs.

The basic driving force of the child is his striving to find a secure place with those people important to him. Mother's influence is unique, for she is generally the most significant person in the young child's life.

The Importance of Past History and Biological Characteristics

There is a great debate raging in psychological circles concerning the importance of past history and biological characteristics. According to the Freudians and some Behaviorists these two things, biological characteristics and past experience, determine behavior. Man, they conclude, is nothing more than a mechanical robot. For members of the Church this conclusion is untenable because it cancels out the creative will of man.

The psychological position taken in this book assumes that past experiences and biological characteristics provide possibilities and probabilities for behavior. They are *not* determiners. The inherited qualities of a child and his past experiences are much less important than what he does with what he has.

There is danger in teaching that biological characteristics and past experiences are the determiners of behavior. Parents who teach this to their children encourage them in the ways of irresponsibility, for they can excuse their misbehavior by arguing, "You are to blame. I cannot help myself."

Free Will, Choice, and Creativity

We who lived in concentration camps can remember the men who walked through the huts comforting others, giving away their last piece of bread. They may have been few in number, but they offer sufficient proof that everything can be taken from a man but one thing: the last of the human freedoms — to choose one's attitude in any given set of circumstances, to choose one's own way.

And there were always choices to make. Every day, every hour, offered the opportunity to make a decision, a decision which determined whether you would or would not submit to those powers which threatened to rob you of your very self, your inner freedom; which determined whether or not you would become the plaything of circumstance, renouncing freedom and dignity to become molded into the form of the typical inmate.

Seen from this point of view, the mental reactions of the inmates of a concentration camp must seem more to us than the mere expression of certain physical and sociological conditions. Even though conditions such as lack of sleep, insufficient food and various mental stresses may suggest that the inmates were bound to react in certain ways, in the final analysis it becomes clear that the sort of person the prisoner became was the result of an inner decision, and not the result of camp influences alone. Fundamentally, therefore, any man can, even under such circumstances, decide what shall become of him — mentally and spiritually. . .*

The above quotation comes from Viktor E. Frankl's book, *Man's Search For Meaning,* and is his interpretive observations of a prisoner of war camp during World War II. It is his hypothesis that regardless of how structured the environment, man does have some control over himself.

INVICTUS

Out of the night that covers me,
Black as the pit from pole to pole,
I thank whatever gods may be
For my unconquerable soul.

In the fell clutch of circumstance
I have not winced nor cried aloud.
Under the bludgeonings of chance
My head is bloody, but unbowed.

Beyond this place of wrath and tears
Looms but the horror of the shade,
And yet the menace of the years
Finds and shall find me unafraid.

It matters not how straight the gate,
How charged with punishment the scroll
I am the master of my fate:
I am the captain of my soul.

William Ernest Henley

The question of whether or not man has free will, the ability to make choices and decisions, has been a basic philosophical controversy down through the recorded history of man. It has not been resolved by philosophical reasoning nor has it been resolved through empirical laboratory processes. In this area man makes his decision based on faith. If he chooses to believe that man is not free, he will tend to fatalism, pessimism, and possibly irresponsibility.

It is the author's assumption that man does have freedom to make choices and decisions within rather broad limits. Therefore, it is proposed not only that the child is being influenced by others in his environment — whether it be in the home or school — but that he is also creatively influencing others. He is an *active agent*, not a passive receiver of stimuli. Not only is Mother training the child, but he is often training her, and sometimes much more effectively than she is training him.

The Child Is Socially Rooted

The child cannot really be understood unless he is considered as an individual who is socially embedded. All important life problems and important life values involve relationships with other people. This concept is beautifully stated in Romans, Chapter 13, verse 9. ". . . if there be any other commandment, it is briefly comprehended in this saying, namely, Thou shalt love thy neighbour as thyself." "Others" is the most important single factor in living. Mother, as she attempts to understand the child, must look at social interactions in order to help him more effectively.

"Life Style" of the Child

The small child first behaves in a rather trial and error-random fashion. He then makes interpretations of his experiences, looking for guiding principles to live by. It appears that these guiding principles become rather firmly established during the ages of two to five and are rather difficult to change after this time. It is as if he were to grind and color his own eyeglasses. These he wears throughout life and all he perceives is filtered through them. This becomes his biased perception. His biased perceptions and related ways of behaving are his life style.

His perceptions and their interpretations may be logical or illogical. The important thing, however, is that the child bases his decisions on them as if they were true and logical even when they are not. When the interpretations are illogical, the child tends to fulfill his own prophecy. An example of this is the child who grows up feeling that life and people are unfair to him. He anticipates the unfairness of others and often hurts them "before they hurt me." As a result, people tend to avoid him or strike back. The child then says to himself, "Yeh, I'm right, people treat me unfairly."

The child whose life style suggests that others do not consider him important may go through life trying to make others feel sorry for him. He may have a martyr complex or react as if he has moral superiority over others whom he considers physically and socially stronger.

It is proposed that if Mother is to understand her child, she must understand the life style that he has built for himself. She should be able to wear the child's colored glasses through which he perceives and interprets his world.

Social Interest

Social interest has reference to the child's ability to cooperate, to be concerned with the welfare of others and to belong to their groups. It includes the capacity to "give and take" and to respect the rules of society. Social interest is seen as a general, positive movement with and among people. Social interest suggests that we view one another as children of God with certain basic rights.

Possibly the best substitute word for social interest is cooperation. The opposite to social interest or cooperation is competition. In competition we tend to move either against or away from people. In contrast to horizontal-cooperative relationships we find the vertical-competitive relationships.

The family that is experiencing difficulties usually exhibits competition among the children for a favored place with the significant members of the family, especially Mother. They may hurt one another, cut one another down, and try to discourage one another as they climb up the vertical ladder to find their choice, favored place.

Social interest is something that is innate with every individual. To grow and develop, however, it must be nurtured. The development of social interest is either encouraged or discouraged primarily by the relationship experiences of the child with those important to him.

The amount of social interest an individual child has greatly influences the extent of his success and happiness in living the full life. If the child has a high level of social interest, he will attempt to understand and observe society's rules. He will respect himself and the rights of others. He will be able to solve new social problems as they confront him. The child with high social interest will be polite, obedient, industrious, honest, modest, and self-reliant. A method for measuring the child's social interest level is to evaluate his ability to cooperate and his willingness to respect society's rules even when it involves personal sacrifice.

It is proposed that parents be concerned with the level of their child's social interest. Much in society discourages its development and encourages its reverse. Society seems to say the only way to get ahead in life — to find success — is to cut others down. This idea is first learned in the competitive family where the child feels that the only way he can find a place is to obtain it at the expense of his brothers and sisters.

The "Wholistic" Nature of the Child

Mother should look upon the child as being "wholistic." The word "wholistic" has reference to the fact that the child must be viewed in his entirety. He is an indivisible whole and cannot be thoroughly understood until this wholeness is accepted. He must be seen in his totality. Some psychological positions have suggested that a person can only be understood as his very small parts are understood. The theory underlying this book is the proposal that all parts are inter-related and interact to effect and make up the whole. Understanding is not encouraged by atomistic and reductive systems. If Mother is to truly understand the child, she must be able to see him functioning as a unique, total entity.

The Family Constellation (Order of Birth)

One of the most fascinating approaches to understanding children is knowing how their order of birth influences them. The order of birth greatly determines the kind of environment in which the child finds himself. The family is a small society in which each person in the family influences the others and is influenced by them. This takes on significance when we recall our assumption that the basic striving of all people is to find a place of belonging. In happy homes we generally find a spirit of cooperation in which the relationships are on a horizontal level. Each has a place in the family, one not dependent upon others having an inferior station. In contrast to this, unhappy families exhibit a spirit of competition, where the child feels he has a place in the family only if other members are farther away from Mother's affections than he. *It is in competitive families that birth order takes on added significance.* The influence of birth order or personality is affected by such factors as sex differences and age spread. The personality of the child can be greatly influenced by his brothers and sisters or lack of them, their ages, and their sexes.

The First Born

This child is often called the dethroned child. He is a first and only child who has had love and attention lavished on him by a young mother. He experiences himself for two or three years as being the major object of concern and care. Suddenly, a younger sibling arrives. His mother's affections and concerns are sharply shifted. He must now learn to share her attention with someone else, a new baby who becomes a rival. He feels dethroned. Because of his experiencing a sudden loss of involvement with Mother, the eldest often goes through life semiconsciously feeling that this kind of thing can happen again. The feeling often stays with him as an adult and influences the way he functions on the job and in his social relationships, including marriage.

If he has experienced a lot of pampering or undue attention as an only child, the eldest often develops hostile feelings toward the second child. He tends to be past-oriented. He looks on the past with favor because it was there he experienced his greatest happiness. He also tends to be protective of others who are suffering, for he identifies with them because he feels that he, also, is hurt and suffering. The first born tends to be conservative and to be oriented along the lines of rules and authority. He looks to authority and rules because he sees in them a protection of his position. He does not care to take chances in life because of fear that he might once again be hurt.

The Middle Child

He is often more active than the oldest. His activity can be either of a constructive or a destructive nature, good or bad. However, if the oldest child tends to be active, the middle child will tend to be less active. Whatever the situation, the first and second child tend to be dissimilar in personality. The middle child tends to feel that he has to make up for lost time. He acts as if he were in a race, moving under full steam. Often the middle child, in a competitive family, will feel slighted or abused. He will feel that people are unfair to him, for he does not have the rights of the older child nor the privileges of the younger. Sometimes he sets his goals so high that it is impossible for him to achieve them, and therefore suffers for the rest of his life by feelings of incapability.

The middle child tends to be revolutionary, subtle, and liberal oriented. This orientation stems from his conviction that he will find his place only through change and revoluton, i.e., by overthrowing the first born. The middle child may have a tendency to slander others, to cut them down, or else to praise them so highly that they cannot possibly meet his verbalized expectations. Through subtlety this child then is able to knock the person off the pedestal upon which he has set him.

The Youngest Child

The youngest seems to be the favored child in history books and fairy tales. It is the youngest who overcomes the older brothers. He rides the white horse. He is the good son. We also find this in religious history as portrayed in the stories of Joseph, David and Nephi .

Typically, the youngest child is the one who is most pampered. He becomes very adroit in manipulating service from others. He is often courageous, for he sees others ahead of him fail; therefore, failure is not such a traumatic thing for him.

The youngest, because he is the smallest and most incapable, may suffer from extreme inferiority feelings. He may have the urge to put himself forward, to advance and to outdo all other people. He becomes adroit and inventive. Often he develops a repertoire of tricks to mask his situation of being the smallest and most incompetent in the family. The tricks typically revolve around getting other people to give him service, which gives him a feeling of importance. He may learn to be a charmer and is able to bring others to him through his cuteness.

So strong is the influence of the family constellation on the child that it is found that the life styles of the youngest children in two different families are usually more alike than the oldest and youngest children of the same family.

The Only Child

This child tends to be in a uniquely disadvantageous position. He is often excessively pampered by a mother who focuses all her attention and service on him alone, the only object which evidences her motherhood. He is the center of attention and soon acts as if this were his right. He grows up expecting life to come to him with no effort on his part.

Mothers of only-children are often found to be afraid of the expenses or possible ill health associated with having other babies. They tend to be pessimistic and unsure of themselves and raise only children who imitate these qualities of pessimism, timidity and lack of self-confidence. The family atmosphere is one of anxiety. Mother stresses the calamities of the environment and her inability to overcome them. The only child imitates his mother. Anxiety and timidity become his stance also. He tends to grow into a discouraged, anxious adult who does not feel that he is worthwhile or competent to master his environment.

This child is often frightened of the possibilities of having brothers and sisters because they would be a threat to his dependent uniqueness in the family situation.

In summary, only-children are often found to be dependent, afraid of being able to cope successfully with their environment, and resentful of others whom they perceive as potential rivals to their unique position.

Other Situations

There are other sibling situations that should be mentioned at this time. A boy in a family of girls is often found to be very strong and masculine or very weak and feminine. The reverse is true for a girl in a family of boys. The influences are kaleidoscopic, depending upon ages, sex, numbers, and the emotional climate between mothers and fathers and the expectations they have for their children. The family institution provides unlimited opportunities for reciprocal discouragement when competiton is emphasized and the children feel that they can belong only by cutting down their brothers and sisters, or pushing them away from their parents. The vertical-competitive relationship seems to be the typical operational pattern of families in difficulty.

It is often found that the prominence of one child becomes a shadow over the other children and tends to discourage them. The good child is often good at the expense of the others, for he is often found to manipulate the environment so that others look bad. The greater activity of one child results in greater inactivity of the one next to him in age. The child who is academically excellent often uses this as a weapon to cut his brothers and sisters down. A child with good looks and physical excellence tends to overshadow his brothers and sisters, especially if Mother dwells on such qualities. On the other hand, the family also provides unlimited opportunities for mutual encouragement when cooperation is emphasized and each is made to feel he has a secure place.

Mother should be somewhat aware of the importance of family constellation if she is to better discipline and train her children.

Maladjustment

The child's difficulties and misbehavior are rooted in his feeling of not belonging. There is nothing more painful for him than his feelings of being excluded from the family. The child who believes he does not belong develops deep feelings of inferiority. Feeling inferior is a tendency for almost all children because they are less competent and smaller physically than those around them; however, mothers who pamper their children stimulate a deeper feeling of inferiority and incompetency. Mothers who have for their children aspirations that are too high or put too many obstacles in their way also stimulate these feelings.

Mothers who idolize or humiliate their children tend to stimulate feelings of insecurity. Children who are idolized are indulged and pampered. The child usually interprets this to mean he is incompetent and cannot do things for himself. He then feels hurt and rebellious. Mothers who humiliate their children usually do it through harsh criticism. They expect too much, and the child responds to others with hurt, rebellion and nonconformity. In both situations the child is discouraged. He feels that he does not have a secure place with those who are important to him.

Biological deformities also tend to bring about feelings of inferiority among children. Children who are crippled, sickly, or ugly tend to feel inferior. These situations are often made worse through faulty training by parents. If they are not spoiled and pampered, there is a tendency for them to overcome their biological handicaps.

When the child feels inferior, there is a tendency for him to turn from moving towards people in a socially integrated, cooperative manner, to moving away or against them through social superiority and competition. The child who responds in this way may attempt to chip away at the pedestals on which he puts others.

It is proposed that the child's faults are miscalculated efforts on his part to get ahead or to rise above other people. He rebels first against his parents, then educators, and then against rules and regulations of society in general.

In summary, misbehavior of the maladjusted child is a result of his feelings of inferiority. He feels that behaving constructively will not get him a secure place with those important to him. Because of his discouragement and faulty perception, he feels that he can find a place only by rising above others, by discrediting them, or, if he is exceptionally discouraged, by withdrawing. Competition is thus emphasized and vertical relationships solidified.

The child who acts constructively is courageous. He feels he can have a place within the family by responding constructively. He tends to cooperate with others and relates on a horizontal plane. He feels that his acceptance is not dependent on others not being accepted. He feels solidarity with mankind. This is based on his assurance that he is accepted by those important to him.

The child's feelings about himself are related to the evaluation that Mother puts on him. If she has faith and trust in him and expresses this through actions by encouraging his independence and competencies, the child will tend to have feelings of well-being toward himself and others.

The A B C D Goals of Misbehavior

Misbehavior of the child is the result of discouragement. He feels he does not have or cannot find a secure place of belonging with Mother or other significant members of the family by acting constructively; therefore, he acts unconstructively and/or destructively. In order for mothers to understand their discouraged children, it is essential that they understand the goals or purposes of their misbehavior. These goals are referred to as the A B C D goals of misbehavior. They are only briefly mentioned here since they are discussed in detail in Chapter VI. However, it should be remembered that the child is usually *not consciously aware* of his goals of misbehavior.

The goals of the misbehaving child are:

A. to get Attention — keep Mother busy with him.

B. to Boss Mother — to have power over her.

C. to Counterhurt — hurt Mother because he feels he has been hurt, get revenge, sometimes called "power with revenge."

D. to appear Disabled — get Mother to assume this.

REFERENCES

Ansbacher, Heinz L. and Rowena R. Ansbacher. *The Individual Psychology of Alfred Adler*. New York: Basic Books, Inc., Publishers, 1956.

Beier, Ernst G. *The Silent Language of Psychotherapy*. Chicago: Aldine Publishing Company, 1966.

Chaplin, J. P. and T. S. Krawiec. *Systems and Theories of Psychology*. New York: Holt, Rinehart, and Winston, 1960.

Dinkmeyer, Don and Rudolph Dreikurs. *Encouraging Children to Learn: The Encouragement Process*. Englewood Cliffs: Prentice-Hall, Inc., 1963.

Dreikurs, Rudolph. *The Challenge of Parenthood*. New York: Duell, Sloan and Pearce, 1958.

Dreikurs, Rudolph. *Psychology in the Classroom, a Manual for Teachers*. New York: Harper and Row, Publishers, 1957.

Frankl, Viktor. *Man's Search for Meaning, an Introduction to Logotherapy*. New York: Washington Square Press, Inc., 1965.

Glasser, William. *Reality Therapy, A New Approach to Psychiatry*. New York: Harper and Row, Publishers, 1965.

Hall, Calvin S. and Gardner Lindzy. *Theories of Personality*. New York: John Wiley and Sons, Inc., 1957.

Henley, William Ernest. "Invictus," *One Thousand Quotable Poems*. Compiled by T. C. Clark and E. A. Gillespie. Chicago: Willett, Clark, and Company, 1937.

CHAPTER III.

The Religious Foundation

Religious beliefs have always had a strong impact on the devout mother, influencing her thoughts and behavior in all phases of her own life as well as the manner in which she raises her children. The purpose of this chapter is to help Mother clarify those religious principles that have important bearings on the understandings and techniques she uses in training and disciplining her children.

Who Is Man

There is no concept of man more noble than that expressed in the following passages:

> That by him, [i.e., Christ] through him, and of him, the worlds are and were created, and the *inhabitants thereof are begotten sons and daughters unto God.* (D&C 76:24)
>
> Man was also in the beginning with God. Intelligence, or the light of truth, was not created or made, neither indeed can be. (D&C 93:29)

From these significant scriptures, we learn about two important characteristics of man. First, that man is a begotten son of God; and second, that his individuality or intelligence is coeternal with God.

> Furthermore we have had fathers of our flesh which corrected us, and we gave them reverence: shall we not much rather be in subjection unto the *Father of spirits,* and live? (Hebrews 12:9)
>
> For in him we live, and move, and have our being; as certain also of your own poets have said, For we are also his offspring.
>
> Forasmuch then as we are the offspring of God . . . (Acts 17:28-29)

Paul, in his epistle to the Hebrews, explicitly stated that man is the spiritual child of God the Father.

From the first two scriptures we learn that man always existed in the eternities. The last two inform us that man, at some time in the past, was clothed by our Father in Heaven with a spiritual body, which made him a begotten spiritual son of God the Father; therefore, man has great dignity and worth.

Purposes of Human Existence

The world is not aware of man's potential grandeur. "Where did man come from?" "Why is he here?" and "Where is he going?" are questions that philosophers and self-styled religionists of all ages have attempted to answer. There is much scepticism in today's world concerning the very existence of God. In Western society it has become fashionable to proclaim that God is dead, dead as to the very existence of God or dead as to God's interest in man and this world. These phrases are even proclaimed from the mouths of men who have dedicated themselves to interpreting the word of God to their fellowman.

It is only through present day revelation that man has a more accurate and complete knowledge of the reality of God and the reasons for man's existence. There are two major purposes for man's mortal existence. First, he is here to work out his own salvation, to train and mold himself.

> And we will prove them herewith, to see if they will do all things whatsoever the Lord their God shall command them; (Abraham 3:25)
> And, if you keep my commandments and endure to the end . . . (D&C 14:7)

The second purpose is to obtain a physical body of flesh and bone.

> For man is spirit. The elements are eternal, and spirit and element, inseparably connected, receive a fulness of joy:
> And when separated, man cannot receive a fulness of joy. (D&C 93:33-34)

And Joseph Smith preached:

> We came to earth that we might have a body and present
> it pure before God in the celestial kingdom. The great principle
> of happiness consists in having a body. The devil has no body,
> and herein is his punishment . . . (Burton, p. 118)

For some reason that mortal man does not thoroughly
understand, it is necessary that his intelligence and spiritual
body be clothed with a body of flesh and bone for his eternal
happiness to be complete. The spirits who had taken possession of the body of a man "dwelling among the tombs,"
gave evidence of the importance of having a body when
they plead with Christ to let them inhabit even the bodies
of a herd of swine located nearby (Mark 5:2-7).

> Adam fell that men might be; and men are, that they
> might have joy. (2 Nephi 2:25)

From the above we learn that an important objective of our
earth life is to live in such a manner that we have joy,
a joy which exists now and will increase in the eternities.
This is achieved through conforming our lives to Gospel
principles.

Why is it important for man to progress and develop
in this earth life? Why the effort to "be ye therefore perfect,
even as your Father which is in heaven is perfect"? (Matt.
5:48). Latter-day revelation has helped answer this question.

> When the Savior shall appear we shall see him as he is.
> We shall see that he is a man like ourselves.
>
> And that same sociality which exists among us here will
> exist among us there, only it will be coupled with eternal glory,
> which glory we do not now enjoy. (D&C 130:1-2)

Joseph Smith taught:

> God himself was once as we are now, and is an exalted
> man, and sits enthroned in yonder Heavens! That is the great
> secret. If the veil were rent today, and the great God who holds
> the world in its orbit, and who upholds all worlds and all things
> by his power, was to make himself visible — I say, if you were

to see him today, you would see him like a man in form. . . .
(Burton, p. 10)

We are of the "sociality" of the Gods. We are His spiritual
children and heirs. In order to be worthy to become His
heirs we must mold ourselves into beings who will eventually,
in the eternities, become perfect as He is now.

God has told us through modern revelation of the great
opportunities that await us.

> And, if you keep my commandments and endure to the end
> you shall have eternal life, [life with God — a life like God's],
> which gift is the greatest of all the gifts of God. (D&C 14:7)
> They are they who are the church of the Firstborn.
> They are they . . . Father has given all things . . .
> Wherefore, as it is written, they are gods, even the sons
> of God.
> Wherefore, all things are theirs, whether life or death, or
> things present, or things to come, all are theirs and they are
> Christ's, and Christ is God's.
> And they shall overcome all things. (D&C 76: 54-55, 58-60)
> Then shall they be gods, because they have no end; there-
> fore shall they be from everlasting to everlasting, because they
> continue . . . (D&C 132:20)

And so we learn that man, if he progresses sufficiently in
this life, will be able to inherit his rightful place in the
eternities with his Father in heaven, having the powers and
rights of godhood including an eternal or continual increase
of spirit children. Man will become a partner working
with God:

> For behold, this is my work and my glory — to bring to
> pass the immortality and eternal life of man. (Moses 1:39)

The godhood potential of her child should be foremost
in Mother's thoughts as she trains and disciplines him.

The Fundamental Principle: Free Agency

David O. McKay, a beloved President of the Church
and long-time apostle of the Lord, spoke these words:

> Next to the bestowal of life itself, the right to direct that
> life is God's greatest gift to man . . . pressing for attention and

action of all liberty-loving people is the preservation of individual liberty. Freedom of choice is more to be treasured than any possession earth can give . . .

Free agency is the impelling source of the soul's progress. It is the purpose of the Lord that man become like him. In order for man to achieve this it was necessary for the Creator first to make him free . . . (*Gospel Ideals,* p. 299)

It is ironic that in our nation where freedom is greatly prized, there are many individuals who have fewer opportunities to practice their free agency than many of those in bondage to their dictatorial states. It is generally better for the individual to experience tyranny from a distant government than to be subjected to tyranny from close family members. Chronic state influences are seldom as pervasive as are those affecting children subjected to tyrannical parents or parents subjected to tyrannical children.

Most, if not all, religious problems are, in the final analysis, social problems. Religious problems in the main are concerned with man's humanity or inhumanity to man. Man's interaction with man is the focus. Evidence of this can be found by quickly checking the Ten Commandments where it is discovered that seven of the ten directly or indirectly relate to men interacting one with another. This is further evidenced by the major purpose of Godhood; "For this is my work and my glory — to bring to pass the immortality and eternal life of man" (Moses 1:39). This work of Godhood implies interaction among men and interaction between God and men. Man will probably be judged for exaltation primarily on the basis of how well he related to his fellowmen.

Master, which is the great commandment in the law?

Jesus said unto him, Thou shalt love the Lord thy God with all thy heart, and with all thy soul, and with all thy mind.

This is the first and great commandment.

And the second is like unto it, Thou shalt love thy neighbour as thyself.

On these two commandments hang all the law and the prophets. (Matt. 22:36-40)

What is the underlying principle that should be man's guide in his relations with others? It is the author's position that it is the eternal principle of free agency. A war was fought in heaven to preserve it (Revelation 12:1-11, Moses 4:3). The United States has fought in two major world wars and numerous smaller ones for the stated purpose of protecting our democratic way of life, which in turn protects the rights of man to practice his free agency. Whereas many of us in America can appreciate and fight for this principle at the state, national, and international level, we are too frequently indifferent or confused at the familial level, where having or lacking free agency usually has the most impact.

It seems reasonable to propose that we take a closer look at one of God's best known suggestions, namely, that we do unto others as we would have others do unto us (Matthew 7:12). If this recommendation were truly followed we would have mutual respect one for another. We would not impose or restrict another's free agency as long as he did not infringe upon the free agency of others. The assumption is that man's interaction with his fellowman is a major, if not the major, concern of God and that the basic principle underlying this interaction is the free agency of each individual.

The Lord has time and again sought to impress on our minds the significance of this principle. The following are quotations from ancient and modern prophets:

> Wherefore, because that Satan rebelled against me, *and sought to destroy the agency of man,* which I, the Lord God, had given him, and also, that I should give unto him mine own power; by the power of mine Only Begotten, I caused that he should be cast down. (Moses 4:3)
>
> For the earth is full, and there is enough and to spare; yea, I prepared all things, and *have given unto the children of men to be agents unto themselves.* (D&C 104:17)
>
> And now remember, remember, my brethren, that whosoever perisheth, perisheth unto himself; and whosoever doeth iniquity, doeth it unto himself; for behold, *ye are free;* ye are permitted to act for yourselves; for behold, God hath given

unto you a knowledge and he hath made you free. (Helaman 14:30)

Therefore, cheer up your hearts, and remember that *ye are free to act* for yourselves — to choose the way of everlasting death or the way of eternal life. (2 Nephi 10:23)

There exists an eternal law that each human soul shall shape its own destiny. No one individual can make happiness or salvation for another. 'Even God could not make men like himself without making them free.' (Gospel Ideals, p. 300)

Brigham Young had the following to say:

My independence is sacred to me — it is a portion of that same Deity that rules in the heavens. There is not a being upon the face of the earth who is made in the image of God, who stands erect and is organized as God is, that should be deprived of the free exercise of his agency so far as he does not infringe upon others rights . . . (Gospel Ideals, p. 300)

President David O. McKay insisted:

. . . There cannot be happiness without free agency. If the soul feels circumscribed, harrassed, or enslaved by something or somebody, there cannot be true progress . . . God intends men to be free. (Gospel Ideals, p. 491)

The Lord has cautioned all of us as we interact with our fellowmen that:

We have learned by sad experience that it is the nature and disposition *of almost all men,* as soon as they get a little authority, as they suppose, they will immediately begin to exercise *unrighteous dominion.* (D&C 121:39)

Not only has the Lord cautioned us about the tendencies of all of us to infringe upon the rights of others, but he has given us some positive suggestions:

No power or influence can or ought to be maintained by virtue of the priesthood, only by persuasion, by long-suffering, by gentleness and meekness, and by love unfeigned;

By kindness, and pure knowledge, which shall greatly enlarge the soul without hypocrisy, and without guile —

Reproving betimes with sharpness, when moved upon by the Holy Ghost; and then showing forth afterwards an increase of love toward him whom thou hast reproved, lest he esteem thee to be his enemy. (D&C 121:41-43)

The importance of having the children of God preserve their free agency cannot be overemphasized. Without it man cannot be truly happy. Without it he cannot progress. Wars have been fought and sanctioned by God for the purpose of preserving liberties so that man might be able to exercise his free agency. This is a main refrain in the Book of Mormon. Moroni inspired the Nephites to battle the Lamanites with ". . . thoughts of their lands, their liberty, yea, their freedom from bondage" (Alma 43:48).

It seems reasonable to assume that every family unit should jealously guard the right of each family member to exercise (practice) the use of his free agency so long as he does not interfere with the rights of others. This is a fundamental principle for guiding the interaction of family members. It is the author's belief that the transgression by parents and/or children of this basic, eternal principle is at the root of most difficulties found in families. If all of us could only learn to truly "do unto others as you would have others do unto you," we would behave towards one another with mutual respect and the by-product, love, would follow.

One of the purposes of this book is to give mothers some specific suggestions for training and disciplining children without destroying their free agency.

Man's Responsibility to Himself

Man's purpose in this life is to enlarge himself by growing in knowledge and understanding of himself and others, and to cope effectively with the vicissitudes of life. This requires that children be raised to have the courage to risk, which is a prerequisite to growth. An illustration of man's responsibility to courageously progress is given in the Savior's parable of the talents.

For the kingdom of heaven is as a man travelling into a far country, who called his own servants, and delivered unto them his goods.

And unto one he gave five talents, to another two, and to another one; to every man according to his several ability; and straightway took his journey.

Then he that had received the five talents went and traded with the same, and made them other five talents.

And likewise he that had received two, he also gained other two.

But he that had received one went and digged in the earth, and hid his lord's money.

After a long time the lord of those servants cometh, and reckoneth with them.

And so he that had received five talents came and brought other five talents, saying, Lord, thou deliveredst unto me five talents: behold, I have gained beside them five talents more.

His lord said unto him, Well done, thou good and faithful servant: thou hast been faithful over a few things, I will make thee ruler over many things: enter thou into the joy of thy lord.

He also that had received two talents came and said, Lord, thou deliveredst unto me two talents: behold, I have gained two other talents beside them.

His lord said unto him, Well done, good and faithful servant; thou hast been faithful over a few things, I will make thee ruler over many things: enter thou into the joy of thy lord.

Then he which had received the one talent came and said, Lord, I knew thee that thou art an hard man, reaping where thou hast not sown, and gathering where thou hast not strawed:

And I was afraid, and went and hid thy talent in the earth: lo, there thou hast that is thine.

His lord answered and said unto him, Thou wicked and slothful servant, thou knewest that I reap where I sowed not, and gather where I have not strawed:

Thou oughtest therefore to have put my money to the exchangers, and then at my coming I should have received mine own with usury.

Take therefore the talent from him, and give it unto him which hath ten talents.

For unto every one that hath shall be given, and he shall have abundance: but from him that hath not shall be taken away even that which he hath.

And cast ye the unprofitable servant into outer darkness: there shall be weeping and gnashing of teeth. (Matt. 25:14-30)

Note that Christ is talking about entrance into the kingdom of heaven. The two courageous men who risked by building on what they had "entered into the joy of the Lord," and were made "rulers over many things." However, one servant did not live courageously. He was so afraid to risk what little he did have that he buried his talent and was, therefore, cast out as an unprofitable servant.

Is our home atmosphere such that we are raising courageous children who have learned to make decisions, accept responsibility, and enjoy a full life? Are we raising those who will enter the kingdom of our Father in heaven? Or are we raising children who are so discouraged that, being afraid to risk, they bury their talents? Are they afraid to make decisions and accept responsibility?

The Lord's admonition to Oliver Cowdery gives additional light on man's responsibility to himself. Brother Cowdery thought he could translate the plates with no effort on his part; however, in the Lord's statement to him, we learn that he had to put forth effort; otherwise he could not translate.

> Behold, you have not understood; you have supposed that I would give it unto you, when you took no thought save it was to ask me.
>
> But, behold, I say unto you, that you must study it out in your mind; then you must ask me if it be right, and if it is . . . (D&C 9:7-8)

Our salvation is dependent on our walking hand in hand with God. We cannot sit back and expect God to work out our salvation. We can only progress as long as we put forth the effort.

Is our home atmosphere of such a nature that our children have the courage to put forth the required effort for continued progress, or do they sit back, afraid to risk growing because they will have some failures?

Man's responsibility to himself is to live the courageous life, to keep trying.

And we will prove them (men) herewith, to see if they will do all things whatsoever the Lord their God shall command them;

And they who keep their first estate shall be added upon; and they who keep not their first estate (spirit life) shall not have glory in the same kingdom with those who keep their first estate; and they who keep their second estate (earth life) shall have glory added upon their heads for ever and ever. (Abraham 3:25-26)

If we keep our second estate, progress and grow in courageous living and accepting responsibility as with the men who developed their talents in Christ's parable, we shall have glory added upon our heads forever and ever.

Mothers can do much to encourage or discourage a child in developing a courageous attitude towards effective living. This book includes some specific suggestions to help mothers rear children who will make a courageous commitment to the responsible life.

Responsibility of Parenthood

Christ has told us in latter-day revelation that the family unit is an eternal institution. In referring to marriages performed by his servants which receive the sealing of the Holy Spirit of Promise, Christ said:

. . . ye . . . shall inherit thrones, kingdoms, principalities, and powers . . . glory in all things, as hath been sealed upon their heads, which glory shall be a fullness and a continuation of the seeds forever and ever.

Then shall they be gods, because they have no end; therefore shall they be from everlasting to everlasting, because they continue; then shall they be above all, because all things are subject unto them . . . (D&C 132:19-20)

A part of the blessings of godhood is the ability, in the resurrected state, of procreation. Eternal parenthood is a part of godhood. This God-given ability, which practically all mankind has in mortal life, will be given in the resurrected state to those who prove themselves worthy in mortality.

What are some of the responsibilities of parenthood? Scriptures have given us some general guidelines.

> And they shall also teach their children to pray, and to walk uprightly before the Lord. (D&C 68:28)

> But I have commanded you to bring up your children in light and truth. (D&C 93:40)

> And ye will not have a mind to injure one another . . .

> And ye will not suffer your children that they go hungry, or naked; neither will ye suffer that they transgress the laws of God, and fight and quarrel one with another . . .

> But ye will teach them to walk in the ways of truth and soberness; ye will teach them to love one another, and to serve one another. (Mosiah 4:13-15)

Basically the challenge of motherhood is to provide the atmosphere and training for children that will enable them to return to their Father in heaven as rightful heirs to their birthright, which is eternal (God-like) life. Our elder spiritual brother, Christ, and our Heavenly Father have given us the overall objectives and some guidelines for being effective parents, but they have not given us all the answers. They expect us, as in every other area in life, to search for ways wherein we can better accomplish the God-given objectives of parenthood and through the process of searching, improve ourselves.

> And I give unto you a commandment that you shall *teach one another* the doctrine of the kingdom.

> Teach ye diligently and my grace shall attend you, that you may be instructed more perfectly in theory, in principle, in doctrine, in the law of the gospel, in all things that pertain unto the kingdom of God, that are expedient for you to understand;

> Of things both in heaven and in the earth, and under the earth; things which have been, things which are, things which must shortly come to pass; things which are at home, things which are abroad; the wars and the perplexities of the nations, and the judgments which are on the land; and a knowledge also of countries and of kingdoms. (D&C 88:77-79)

> And, verily I say unto you, that it is my will . . . to obtain a knowledge of history, and of countries, and of kingdoms, of laws of God and man, and all this for the salvation of Zion. Amen. (D&C 93:53)

It is at this point that we turn to some of the teachings of man that can help Mother accomplish the demanding tasks of motherhood. It is the author's intent to provide, in the remaining chapters, information for Mother which correlates with basic religious principles and which will enable her more effectively to rear her children.

REFERENCES

The Book of Mormon. Salt Lake City: The Church of Jesus Christ of Latter-day Saints, Publishers, 1951.

Burton, Alma P. *Discourses of the Prophet Joseph Smith.* Salt Lake City: Deseret Book Company, 1956.

Doctrine and Covenants. Salt Lake City: The Church of Jesus Christ of Latter-day Saints, Publishers, 1951.

The Holy Bible.

The Improvement Era. *Gospel Ideals.* Salt Lake City: The Deseret News Press, 1953.

The Pearl of Great Price. Salt Lake City: The Church of Jesus Christ of Latter-day Saints, Publishers, 1951.

CHAPTER IV.

Principles for Attaining the Objectives

It is anticipated that Mother will want to rear children who as adults will function well in the democratic society and have the courage to progress until they are worthy of an inheritance in the celestial kingdom. Principles for child rearing should insure that these objectives are met. Child rearing practices of totalitarian states, such as Nazi Germany or the present Communist regimes, which want to encourage unhesitating obedience and loyalty to the state, are quite different from those encouraged in the American-Christian home. The author believes that the principles discussed in this chapter foster democratic and Christian principles, ideals, and objectives. Free agency, the worth and value of each soul, and continued progression are among the major concerns.

Some Underlying Principles

Choice

Mother should provide her child with choices at the earliest possible opportunities by giving alternatives whenever she makes a request. An example: "Johnnie, would you like to stop crying or would you like to take your crying to your bedroom?" Mother sets the limits by requesting he either stops crying or takes his crying to his bedroom. But he can make the final choice as to which of these two things he will do.

By allowing and encouraging the child to make choices, Mother respects the free agency of the child and encourages him to be responsible for his own behavior. Some of the values in providing alternatives for the child are: (1) it encourages the child to make decisions and be responsible for them, (2) he will learn to make decisions through practice as encouraged by Mother, and (3) by providing choices for the child, Mother avoids imposing her will, thus side-stepping conflict. The child can move on his own by making the final decision as to what happens to him. Many mothers are caught up in power struggles with their children. Giving the child a choice is an excellent way of avoiding this.

The children can be allowed choices at almost any age and in almost any situation. The boundaries, however, are drawn by Mother. The alternatives are limited according to what she feels she can comfortably live with and the competency and maturity level of the child.

By providing many experiences wherein the child has practice in learning how to make decisions in choice situations, Mother will stimulate growth towards democratic and Church citizenship. Responsible people who have learned to make and to follow through with their decisions are necessary for the survival of democratic states and the efficient functioning of the Church.

One of the tragedies within the Church and American society is the great number of indecisive people who have never learned to commit themselves by making decisions. Counseling services and psychological clinics are flooded with dependent people who give up their lives to others through getting others to make their decisions for them. By providing alternatives for the child as he grows and learns to cope with the world about him, Mother stimulates growth.

Stimulate Independence

Many mothers, upon seeing their nine or ten-month-old baby totter and fall, bump heads with visiting relatives as they scramble to be the first to reach the child. This stimulates dependence when independence is so desirable for the health and happiness of the individual and the well-being of the Church and society. It would contribute far more toward fostering independence if Mother and relatives, rather than trying to race one another to protect the child, would stay where they are and encourage the child with words such as, "You can get up by yourself," "Keep trying." Reaching over, picking him up and asking him if he is hurt tends to bring about feelings that "I'm not good enough. I can't cope with life." *training mother*

A mother who has her own self-worth tied to doing things for the child becomes victim to encouraging the child to depend and rely upon her rather than upon himself. The child becomes an adult who is afraid he can handle neither his environment nor himself. He leans on others. The concomitant feelings that develop are worthlessness, inadequacy and dissatisfaction with himself and with life in general.

Mother has many opportunities to encourage independence in even the very young. The mother who encourages her child to walk even though he acts hurt is encouraging independence. She who allows the child to settle his quarrels with his neighborhood friends without her interfering is encouraging independence. She who lets the child dress himself, even though his shoes are on the wrong feet and his shirt is on backwards, is encouraging independence. The areas in which Mother has opportunities for encouraging and stimulating independence are as vast as the experiencial world of the child and her imagination to make use of them.

Stimulate Courageousness in the Child

Mother's general attitude toward the child has a great impact on his level of courage for coping with life. The mother who has faith and trust in her child will generally raise a child who has faith and trust in himself. The child tends to adopt for himself the attitudes his parents have towards him. If Mother dislikes the child, doesn't think he can do anything good enough, feels that he is worthless and no good, the child soon learns to adopt these same feelings for himself. By contrast, if Mother has faith that the child can accomplish, is of worth and lovable, can be trusted and is basically honest, he will tend to meet these expectations and feel that he is a person of value.

At times because of discouragement, the child will attempt to get Mother to feel that he is helpless in order to avoid responsibility. When Mother gives in to pressure from the child by taking the responsibility herself, his feelings of worthlessness are intensified. An example of this is a child who will not make up her mind concerning a particular item of clothing to buy. She looks at her mother communicating, "I am unable to make up my mind." Much frustration and discomfort is usually expressed by the child. Mother immediately comes to the rescue and makes the decision for the child. This kind of behavior on Mother's part says more than words that, "Yes, you are incompetent. You can't make up your mind, so let Mother do it for you." Mother's feeding into these manipulations of the child stimulates discouragement.

Another problem of some mothers is that of setting their standards for the child too high. If the child feels that his present achievement is too much lower than the high standard set by the mother, he gives up in discouragement and refuses to continue trying. Perfectionistic mothers who demand much of themselves tend to set standards that are too high for their children. This is sometimes especially true of the mother who wants her child to be perfect now. Mother must have the courage to accept imperfections in her child if she is to rear a child who will have the courage to grow and progress continually.

Setting standards too low for the child is also discouraging to him. The mother who has low expectations communicates to the child, "I have little faith or trust in you. I do not think that you can accomplish very much. You are of little value."

Maintaining a proper balance between setting expectations and standards too high or too low for a particular child requires sensitivity in determining where the child is at any given time with regard to his courage and performance levels. The child should always feel that the expectations of Mother are attainable.

Train for Cooperation, Not Competition

A sickness of the day is that of striving to compete against others. It is the concept of getting ahead at the expense of others. People who emphasize competition emphasize the vertical relationship. They tend to relate in a superior-inferior fashion. They see the world as a world of superiors and inferiors, a world of unequals. Their position is continually threatened by those beneath and above them. Theirs is a very insecure world and, therefore, they strive to attain positions above others in order to feel superior. Practically all other men are perceived as potential enemies, whom they then respond to as such. They do not understand that their progression is relatively independent of the progress of others. Our society is full of emotional cripples who relate to their fellowmen in the vertical fashion.

An alternative is to train our children to see the world as a place of equals where there is a place for everyone. Competition in such a world is against one's self, not against others. The object should be to get ahead of one's self, to be a better person today than the person of yesterday. Mother holds a central position in the child's life for encouraging a cooperative outlook towards others. She should train the child to perceive others as truly his brothers and sisters. The key to this view is in the family. He should feel that his belonging in the family is not dependent upon his brothers and sisters being made lower than himself. If Mother succeeds, his view of relationships will tend to be horizontal. He will feel that everyone can belong. A cooperative child can love. He will be a friend to mankind, not an enemy.

Respect the Child

Mother can show respect for her child by remembering consciously that he is a child of God. He is a spiritual brother and is, in a sense, equal before God. Each child has certain inalienable rights, which should be respected. The Golden Rule of, "Do unto others as you would have others do unto you," is just as valid today as it has ever been. There cannot exist love without respect. Mother should respect the right of her child to grow and develop until he is relatively independent of her. This is the child's right as a democratic citizen and as a person with the God-given right to free agency. No person should take advantage of another person. Mother should not take advantage of her child, nor should the child take advantage of Mother.

Train the Child to Respect the Rights of Others

One of the tragedies in American society is that too many mothers are training their children to disrespect the rights of others. Irresponsibility, expecting the world to provide them with a living, and expecting society to entertain them are terms and phrases which can be used to describe too many of our young people and adults. One of the best ways for Mother to train the child to respect the rights of others is to respect herself. Mother should not allow herself to be used by her child as a doormat. She should not do everything for the child nor allow herself to be manipulated by the child into situations which are detrimental to herself and him. An example is that of a twelve-year-old girl continuing to demand that her mother dress her, make her bed, clean up her bedroom and do all the ironing. The mother who gives in to these kinds of demands from her child will be doing two things: (1) training the child to disrespect the rights of others and (2) encouraging irresponsibility and dependency on the part of the child.

Possibly the best method Mother has to induce her child to respect the rights of others is to insist that the child respect her rights. This relationship becomes the exemplary relationship for the child as he moves out into ever-widening circles of friends and acquaintances. If the child's relationship with Mother has been one of mutual respect, he will tend to establish respectful relationships with others.

Train the Child to Respect Order

A certain amount of order is required if relationships among people are to run smoothly and society is to be productive. Society cannot exist in anarchy. It must be orderly for it to be beneficial to the individual as well as to the group. Again, Mother is in a key position to train her child to respect and live in conformance with order. An effective way she has to train her child to respect order is to have an orderly home. A schedule should be established in the home for doing chores, eating, sleeping, studying, and etc.

This does not mean, however, that once a routine is established it is maintained rigidly regardless of the consequences. What is suggested is that the routine be maintained for the benefit of the individual and the group. When a particular routine interferes with the welfare of the family, it should be altered through group action.

Routine and order will not only train the child to respect order and to become used to responding within an orderly society, it will also give him a degree of security because his life will be predictable. A certain amount of order and predictability in the world makes it possible for people to be secure and productive. Life would be chaotic and unproductive if man were not able to develop predictable habits. For example, if every morning before a person could get out of bed he had to think of which foot to put down first, which shoe to put on first and which shoe to tie and how to tie it, he would be a slave to detail. By training the child to develop habits of routine and order, he will be secure, freed from the inconsequential and better able to concentrate on the important things in life.

Rules and regulations, order and routine should be for the benefit of the individual and society. They should not be a prison. They should be seen as devices that give security and free the individual for more meaningful endeavors.

Some Practical First Principles in Successful Child Rearing

Train the Child When the Relationship Is Good

Too much training is attempted during times of conflict when Mother is angry and upset with the child. This is usually not the best time, for there are many more things being learned by the child than are intended by Mother.

An older child three years of age will often poke at a baby sister of seven or eight months. Mother sees this and is afraid that the older child will seriously hurt the younger. A typical reaction is for mother to angrily say to the older, "Don't touch my baby." "You'll hurt her, you naughty boy."

What is being learned by the oldest? First, he may learn one way to get mother upset is to poke the baby. Second, he may think mother is more concerned about the baby than she is about him. Third, he may learn dislike for the baby.

A more effective method for teaching the child is to say nothing, then gently take him away from her and get him involved in something else. At another time Mother could talk to him in a very loving way saying that babies are very little and a big boy like him has to be careful how he handles her because he is older and can do more things.

Mother should make a special effort to train the child at times when there is a good feeling between herself and the child or when feelings are somewhat neutral. A general rule is that training should not take place when there is negative emotion in the relationship or when either child or Mother is upset and angry.

One of the best times to train the child is in the evening when he is in bed and Mother is through with her work for the day. This is a time when Mother can sit on the edge of his bed and assist him to better understand why he is having trouble with the boy down the street, things he might do which would help him to get along better with his sister, how much Mother appreciates his taking out the garbage, etc. Another valuable time for training the child is when Mother is happily involved in work around the house and can bring the child into partnership with her. If she is enjoying baking cookies, she might ask the child if he would like to help her cut them out and put them in the pan. She might also ask him if he would like to assist her in such things as setting the table. There are innumerable opportunities for Mother to train the child by allowing him to cooperate with her.

When Requests Are Made, Make Them Reasonable and Sparse

Very often we find that "a good mother" is a demanding mother. She tends to want perfection in herself and also in her child. She attempts to control the child's every move, a tendency that is diametrically opposed to the eternal principle of free agency. It encourages rebellion and overt hostility or passivity and timidity. Mother's requests of the child should be reasonable. The child should be able to make logical sense out of the request and feel within himself that the requests are reasonable. Requests should be made infrequently. Continual demanding by Mother produces frustration and conflicts between herself and her child. It also tends to produce a dependent adult.

Play Down Bad Habits

If Mother is to encourage the child, she should not constantly voice disapproval of his bad habits. Every child picks up some bad habits. Mother's focusing on them tends to entrench them into the habit repetoire of the child, for Mother's emphasis on the bad keeps them foremost in the child's mind. Also, they may become devices for keeping her busy with him.

It is suggested that Mother eliminate criticism completely from her interaction with the child. Criticism itself results in discouragement. By criticism is meant ridiculing, censuring, or unfavorably expressing judgment of the child's bad habits. Mothers, however, are cautioned not to equate eliminating criticism with doing nothing to change bad habits.

It is also suggested that Mother minimize the mistakes made by both the child and herself. If her energy is spent in emphasizing mistakes, there is little left for changing the bad habits and inducing more positive behavior. Energy should be expended constructively to encourage the child to further progress and development. Emphasizing mistakes and bad habits communicates to the child distrust and little faith which stimulates feelings of worthlessness and "what's the use?"

Pity Has Many Pitfalls

Many a "good mother" is caught in the "pity trap." There are many pressures on mothers to meet the expectations of certain elements in society if they are to be "good mothers." Society tends to pass negative judgments on mothers who do not step in and do things for the children when they are in difficulty. It at times demands that Mother fuss over her child. This is especially true if a child is suffering from a physical or mental handicap. A mother of a child who is blind, who lets him experience some of the hard knocks as he learns to get around in a new environment, often subjects herself to severe criticism from relatives and others who say she is not concerned enough about her child. Mother, even against her better knowledge and understanding, often gives in to those pressures and gives undue service.

Pressure from the child himself is another pressure brought to bear on Mother. A child can learn very early to get Mother to do what he wants for him by looking sad eyed and helpless as he attempts to perform a particular task. This says in effect, "I can't do it; come and do it for me. If you love me, you will do it for me," or "You will get me out of this jam." If Mother is "on the ball" she will respond to the child by saying, "I have confidence in you;

I know that you can do it." Mother shows respect for the child's ability to grow and develop. She gives trust and encouragement which will be adopted by the child as his own.

When we express pity or sympathy for the child we are showing disrespect. Pity says, "You do not have the ability. It's too bad you are so incompetent. Let me, a much more competent person, do it for you."

Pity is a trap. Let mother beware.

Don't Be Panicked by Fears

One of the cases with which the author is acquainted concerned a young adolescent who was sleeping with her mother. When Mother was telling the story, she described how as a little child her daughter had been afraid of the dark. Mother was very concerned and, being afraid of traumatizing the child by making her stay in her room, allowed the child to sleep with her. The girl at the age of thirteen was still sleeping with Mother and Dad was still sleeping on the couch in the living room.

By being impressed and concerned by the child's fears, Mother rewards fear. It is as if she were to say to the child, "When you are fearful, Mother will get upset about you and be very much concerned over you." To the discouraged child this is interpreted as meaning that in order to get Mother most concerned and most involved with him, he must be fearful. A child does not consciously think of this, but it is a semi-conscious process which brings about the desired result: involvement with Mother. How much better it would be for Mother to say to the child, "I understand how you feel, but I know you will get over it." This should be said in a calm, "matter of fact" manner.

In the case of the thirteen year-old fearful girl, a night light would have helped to dispel the fears. Mother's being unafraid and unconcerned about the child's fears would have helped diminish them. When Mother gets upset and anxious over the child's fear it tends to intensify. Fear should be handled with understanding and with faith that the child will get over it. A calm, composed mother can do much to dispel fears of the child and prevent him from learning to use fear to manipulate special attention, service, and concern from her. He will also not learn to use fear to avoid responsibility.

Your Tone of Voice Communicates Too

The words we say communicate only a small part of our total message. Many other things communicate to the child all that we feel and think. Such things are facial expressions, gestures, and especially the tone of voice. The tone of voice can indicate understanding, faith in the child, love, and trust, or it can indicate just the reverse. Mother tends to develop a habitual tone as she deals with trying to correct the misbehavior of the child. Usually it is a tone of displeasure, disgust, or anger. This the child usually responds to with more disturbing behavior. Mother, watch your total communication!

Listen

Mother, it is important that you take time to listen to the total communication of the child so that you can understand him and work with him. Too many "good mothers" talk to the child ninety percent of the time and listen ten percent of the time. It would be better for the relationship and further growth of the child if this could be cut back to about fifty-fifty ratio where Mother is listening half of the time and the child is listening half of the time.

Be Consistent — Follow Through With What You Say and Mean

Mother should develop the habit of not saying anything she does not mean and of consistently following through with what she says. This advice is closely related to a following injunction to stop talking and begin acting. We find that inconsistent mothers are usually mothers who talk much.

A child learns very early whether or not to believe in what his mother says. If Mother does not follow through with what she says, she is encouraging the child to manipulate her, to keep her involved and busy with him. An example of this is the child who is told to eat his dinner or he can't have dessert. The child whose mother does not mean this very readily perceives the hesitancy in her total communication. He tends to dally with his food. Mother finds herself continually nagging the child to hurry up and eat. When dessert comes, she feels sorry for him and gives him dessert even though he is unfinished. Consistency demands he not eat dessert if he does not eat the main course. The child is creative, perceptive, and powerful in being able to manipulate further inconsistency from an inconsistent mother.

Proof of consistency is the sure prediction, on the part of the child, of what Mother will do. For example, if he does not eat his dinner he knows absolutely that Mother will not give him dessert.

Watch Your Pleasing — Be Courageous Enough to Say No

It is suggested by some that one of the greatest problems in American society is that of the pampered child. It takes courage and strength for a mother to say no when the child comes home and says that all the other kids are doing it, or that so and so's mother is letting so and so do it. Sometimes the child will test Mother and, in his own illogical way, feel that if Mother does not say no she does not really love him. Many teen-agers seen by psychologists feel that their mothers don't love them. One of the common reasons given is "Mother will let me do anything that I want." So, Mother, have the courage to say no when it is best for the child.

Keep Social Pressures and All Needs for Prestige from Interfering

As suggested earlier, social pressures too often influence mother negatively as she trains her children. Often these social pressures, when Mother gives into them, encourage irresponsibility on the part of the child. The child who acts helpless in public and demands service from Mother is very often able to manipulate the sentiment of those around him in support of himself and against Mother. It takes courage for Mother to be firm and do what she knows is best for the child regardless of the pressures of well-meaning people around her. The pampered child is especially very sensitive to these pressures on Mother and becomes very adept at using them to his immediate advantage.

The Basic Approach to Misbehavior

Don't "Feed Into" the Misbehaving Child's Goals

Paying off the misbehaving child's expectations usually occurs when Mother responds to him with the first thing that comes to mind. First impulse responses by Mother are the very behaviors the child is manipulating from her, whether they be giving undue service or attention, screaming at the child, crying, avoiding him, or not encouraging his growth and progress.

Basic guidelines for not reinforcing the child's misbehavior are briefly presented below. A more complete discussion is given in Chapter VI where specific suggestions are made.

The Goals	Mother Should:
A. to get *A*ttention	ignore the child.
B. to *B*oss mother, exert power over her.	sidestep the power struggle.
C. to *C*ounterhurt, get revenge.	not show hurt, avoid the struggle.
D. to appear *D*isabled, get mother to think it.	not give up on the child, keep encouraging him to try.

Watch Your Involvement, Mother

Attention and involvement given by Mother to the child should be of such a nature that he behaves more constructively and cooperatively. Too often Mother allows herself to feed the child's unconstructive and sometimes destructive behavior. Unconstructive behavior is that behavior of no real value to the child or family. Destructive behavior interferes with the efficient functioning of the family. The child who demands service from Mother and who keeps her involved in arguments is getting her to feed into his destructive ways. The child who requests compliments and praise in everything he does is unconstructively manipulating Mother to give undue attention. It is suggested that Mother should not get involved with the child in unconstructive or destructive interactions.

Don't Give in to Your First Impulse—Do the Unexpected

When Mother acts upon her first impulse when the child misbehaves, she tends to do the very thing that the child is manipulating from her. Behavior is purposeful. When the misbehaving child gets the response from Mother that he is striving for, she is paying him off for that kind of behavior. This results in a further solidification of the habits that she would rather change, for the child's goal expectations are met. Mother should disengage from the disturbing child by not doing the first thing that comes to her mind. When in doubt, she should do nothing and then later do things which are independent of the manipulations of the child and in conformance with her own training values. Not giving in to her first impulse will help her achieve this.

Choose Natural and Logical Consequences in the Disciplining and Training of Children

In training and disciplining a child, limits have to be set on his behavior and certain consequences must occur if he is to learn to behave within the set limits. It is suggested that rather than using the more traditional techniques with the misbehaving child such as scolding and spanking, Mother use natural and logical consequences.

Natural Consequences

Mother does nothing when using natural consequences. She does not interfere in the child experiencing the natural consequences of his misbehavior. An example is the child who loses a new ball bat. Mother does not run to the store and buy a new one. By not interfering, Mother helps the child to learn that if he is irresponsible in taking care of his bat, he has to do without it for a while. When Mother calls once and the child does not come for supper, the natural consequences are that supper is over and dishes are done. He does not get the kind of supper that was prepared for the rest of the family nor does mother prepare him a special meal. He prepares his own and cleans up his own mess or goes without.

Not doing anything when the child is in difficulty is one of the more difficult things for "good mothers" to learn to do. However, if the child is to be taught responsibility for his own behavior he must be allowed to experience the consequences of his misbehavior. Mother steps in only when there is real danger to the child.

Logical Consequences

These are somewhat different from natural consequences. In logical consequences, Mother structures the environment in such a way that the child experiences the reasonable consequences for his misbehavior. An example of this is the child who is playing in the back yard and runs out into a busy street. Mother can talk to the child and tell him that either he remains in the back yard or he will have to come in the house because of dangers in the road. The logical consequences of his misbehavior in running out into a busy street are that the cannot play in the back yard for the rest of the day. His freedom, which he has abused, is restricted. This is the logical consequence of misuse of freedom.

Another example is the child who continually "bugs" Mother to feed him even though he is capable of feeding himself. The *natural* consequence is for Mother to refuse to feed the child. If he does not feed himself he does not eat. The *logical* consequence is for her to sit away from him at the table if he continues to "bug" her to feed him.

The philosophy behind both natural and logical consequences is that the child experiences the consequences of his misbehavior.

There are certain guidelines that Mother should follow as she uses logical consequences. They are as follows:

1. The consequences are a reasonable result of the misbehavior and are not retaliation or punishment on the part of Mother to get even with or humiliate the child.

2. Choices are provided; for example telling the little boy who insisted on running out in the busy street that he had the choice of staying in the back yard or coming in the house. This way the child determines what will happen to him within limits set by Mother.

3. The results of the consequences are logical and understandable to the child.

4. Mother is to watch her tone of voice. There is a tendency for her, when disturbed by the child, to be angry with him. Her tone of voice should be calm, not angry.

5. Mother is to empathize with the child. She is to know and understand how the child feels; however, she is not to pity or sympathize with him, for this may weaken her resolve and firmness in dealing with him.

It is suggested that rather than using the traditional methods in correcting the misbehavior of children, Mother work at using natural and logical consequences. They tend to encourage a better relationship between her and the child and also encourage him to accept the responsibility for his own actions.

The Time-Out Room

There are times when a powerful child who has experienced much success in defeating, hurting, or tyrannizing Mother cannot be dealt with successfully through immediate, constructive interaction or by Mother's withdrawing from his provocation. A "time-out" room can be very helpful in neutralizing the effects of such a child.

The time-out room has a lock on the door. It is a place where the child can go or be put until he can agree to settle down. It is well-lighted and well-ventilated. There is nothing in it that would concern Mother if it were destroyed. The powerful child will usually increase his forceful, revengeful behavior when he is thwarted in his attempts to tyrannize Mother. His behavior often gets worse before it gets better, for he thinks the reason it is not working now must be because he is not trying hard enough.

These are guidelines which Mother should follow:

1. Before the child is sent to or placed in the room, he is given the choice of settling down or going to the time-out room.

2. If he does not settle down, he has made his choice. Mother is to pick him up gently, but firmly, and place him in the room if he chooses not to go voluntarily.

3. Mother tells him he can come out as soon as he agrees to behave.

4. Mother talks as little as necessary. Her tone of voice is firm but gentle, devoid of anger or hostility.

5. The child is given the choice of staying in the room with the door locked or unlocked. Mother might say, "You can stay in the room with the door unlocked. The door will be locked if you refuse to stay. The decision as to whether mommy locks the door is yours."

6. Mother is to remove the child to the time-out room for his own good, not for retaliation, or for punishment.

Quit Talking and Act

A common problem of mothers who come to family counseling clinics is that they talk-talk-talk to their children rather than act. It seems that one of the reasons for this is that Mother, in her desire to be a good mother and to get the child to feel well towards her, is afraid to act. Talking too much often becomes nagging and this increases the problems between Mother and child.

Children, especially the very young, learn to keep Mother involved by doing mischievious things. Since one of the goals of misbehavior is to keep Mother involved, her talking — a kind of involvement— tends to encourage and reward such behavior. Also, the mother who talk-talks trains the child not to listen.

Mothers should tell the child once and then follow through with firm action if the behavior does not improve.

Limitations

It is the mother's responsibility to set limitations on the behavior of her child. Limitations should be set so that the child feels he is in control of his own life. Limitations should not be so narrow that the child cannot make choices nor should they be so loose that he does not know what is expected and as a result does not feel secure. The child who has few, if any, limits often feels that Mother does not love him since she is not concerned about what he does.

It takes sensitivity on the part of Mother to set boundaries that will allow the child freedom to make choices in his life and yet give him direction for his behavior. A guideline for Mother is that she set boundaries for behavior with which she can live. By this is meant that regardless of what the child chooses to do within the boundaries set by Mother, his behavior will be acceptable to her. An example is the limitations given by Mother to a child playing outside. Let us suppose a child is five years of age and that there is a deep ditch with water in back of the yard. Mother might say, "Johnny, you can play in our yard or you can play in Jimmie's yard. These are the boundaries for your play. But the decision as to just where you play is up to you." Mother is providing a choice for the child, and at the same time she is providing limitations within which the child can safely play. The child can then choose as to whether he plays in his own yard or in his friend's yard; however, he has to make the choice within these limitations. He cannot play along the ditch.

As a child progresses and learns responsible behavior, Mother will find that she can broaden the boundaries and limitations she sets for him until, as an adult, he will have learned to make choices and behave responsibly in order to use profitably the freedom of adulthood. He will also feel secure for he will have adopted a value system for his behavior.

Withdrawal Can Be Very Effective

One of the most effective measures that Mother can use when the child is being provocative or obnoxious is to withdraw from the child's behavior. Mother's calm, quiet withdrawal to another room when the child is upset and angry can be most effective. She may go to the bathroom where she might lock the door, read a book and listen to the radio as she sits out the child's storm. By doing this, Mother does not engage the child at his level of behavior and thus does not feed into or pay off the anger of the child. After the storm has subsided and it is convenient for Mother, she can go to the child and let him know that she cares. This might be in the form of an arm around the shoulder, a hug, a squeeze, or some animated discussion about something on which both are interested.

The reason that withdrawal is so effective is that it gives the child no chance to be rewarded or paid off for his disturbing behavior. Children learn to throw temper tantrums or to be obnoxious for the purpose of getting Mother involved with them. If Mother does not engage with them in this kind of behavior, the payoff is not given and the behavior loses its purpose.

Often "good mothers" have the feeling that if they withdraw from such an engagement with the child, they are losing a battle. Mothers who withdraw are not surrendering to the child. They are simply not allowing the child to manipulate them or engage them in their childlike behavior. It is suggested that good mothers beware of over concern with the child and the feeling that they have to do something every time the child misbehaves. Withdrawal from the misbehavior is similar to a sailing ship riding out a storm. Rather than putting up more sails, the sailors take them down to lessen the effects of the wind. If more sails are put up the boat is driven out of control and possibly wrecked. So it is with mothers who allow themselves to be manipulated by the powerful, disturbing child. Mother gets emotional and upset; the child observes this and is rewarded for his misbehavior. He becomes stimulated to more misbehavior.

Withdraw from the provocative behavior and get involved or busy with the child when he is being cooperative and constructive. Mother can insure that the child does not interpret that she is withdrawing from him as a person by giving him attention and involvement when he is behaving.

Mother, Be Firm With Yourself — Do Not Dominate

One of the problems between Mother and the disturbing child is that in her attempts to correct the misbehavior of the child she tries to control him through her own superiority. Rather than coercing or forcing the child to change his behavior, Mother should be firm with her own behavior. This is a hard concept for many to understand; however, the principle is quite simple. Mother is to keep to the limits she has set for the child. She is firm with herself and does not allow herself to be manipulated by the child into changing the limits. She can do this without dominating the child, for if she allows the child a choice, he can determine what exactly will happen to him. This concept suggests that Mother sets limits and is firm in keeping the limits, but she does not force the child into one specific behavior, for choices are always provided.

When They Fight Treat All As a Group

The modern mother too often gets herself into an impossible situation by getting involved in her childrens' quarrels and disagreements. Mother gets in a position of trying to be judge, jury, and the executioner of her judgment.

It is an impossible way of dealing with fighting children for a number of reasons. First, Mother cannot really be fair because she does not and cannot know all of the circumstances provoking the disagreement. It is often found that where an older and younger child are in disagreement, Mother tends to take a position favoring the younger, for she feels "within her heart" that he cannot stand up for himself against the belligerence and the muscular superiority of the older child. The younger child learns very quickly to manipulate the situation to cause it to appear that he is being abused so that Mother will come to his rescue. This becomes his way of showing his importance to the other children and also proving his worthwhileness and importance to himself, for by manipulating the situation he gets mother to side with him against the others.

A second reason why Mother's involvement in quarrels and fighting should be avoided is to give the children the opportunity to learn to solve difficulties themselves. When Mother goes to his rescue the younger child learns to depend on authority outside himself to meet conflict situations with his fellow men. He needs the experience whereby he can learn to work through problem situations with others.

Third, the older child perceives Mother favoring the younger child at his expense. He says to himself that Mother loves the other child more than she loves him.

And fourth, the children learn very quickly to cooperate in their fighting in order to keep Mother busy with them. This they believe in their own illogical perception, is evidence that Mother cares for them and loves them because she is busy with them rather than busy with household chores and other work.

Whenever children are fighting or quarreling, Mother should treat them as a group and say such things as the following: "Either settle your differences peacefully or go outside and solve them." "Okay, kids, knock it off. I know you can settle it between the two of you." If Mother treats her children as a group when they are experiencing conflicts, she will be saved much nervous and emotional energy. It will make it easier for her to relate with her children in more positive ways with better feelings.

Punishment Should Be Avoided

Traditionally, the approach by Mother has been to punish the child when he misbehaves. By punisment is meant physical or verbal retaliation by Mother. It includes humiliating the child. It may be in the form of spanking, whipping, or verbal ridicule. The typical characteristic of punishment is that it has little or no direct relationship to the child's misbehavior. Practically all research done in the area of punishment has indicated that the results and effects of punishment are unstable, unpredictable and negative.

Some children who are punished severely become withdrawn, timid, and shy, especially towards authority figures; or they become overly aggressive and abusive to others. They tend to develop a philosophy that, "If people have the right to punish me, I have the right to punish others." Often the child who is punished severely becomes submissive to others who can dominate and yet at the same time a bully to those who are weaker than he. He tends to see the world as a place of superiors and inferiors who hurt one another.

Another problem with punishment is that the child tends to equate negative feelings with the one administering the punishment. For example, if Mother punishes severely, the child tends to equate the negative feelings associated with the punishment to his relationship with Mother. Mother, then, takes on what is sometimes called a negative valence. She becomes like the punishment, disliked and sometimes hated.

Punishment can be somewhat effective in stopping or changing one specific misbehavior. However, many other different kinds of behavior are learned in the process. The story comes to mind of a father who was very brutal with three sons. He whipped them with sticks, boards, and leather belts. This continued until they had grown into young men. One day, as they were working in the field, the father lost his temper and began to beat one of the boys. They all turned on him, lashed him to a tree, and thrashed him severely. They then left home, leaving him to die where he was. They had learned hatred and to punish others.

Possibly the main advantage to punishment is that it sometimes makes a mother feel better for it enables her to work off her anger and frustration.

There are better ways of dealing with misbehavior than that of verbal ridicule or the inflicting of physical pain on one weaker than Mother. A better way is the use of natural and logical consequences, which are more effective, help train the child to accept responsibility for his own behavior, and provide for the development of a better relationship with Mother.

Use Care in Rewarding

Rewards are being used by many sophisticated people in attempting to get animals and children to behave in certain ways. This has proved quite effective in some respects. When Mother gives a piece of candy, special privileges, money, etc. to a child in return for his behaving, she is using rewards.

One of the serious problems in using rewards in getting the child to perform is that it trains the child to respond to and value symbols rather than the good behavior itself. Many have confused value systems. They are people who equate the dollar, Cadillac, beautiful home, a prestigious church or professional position, with being good. Symbols become substitutions for good behavior. The person becomes distorted in his values, assuming that simply because he holds tangible symbols of success he is indeed a good or successful person. If Mother wishes to confuse the value system of her child, she is guaranteed success by emphasizing rewards or the symbols of success rather than emphasizing the value of good behavior itself.

Another problem in giving rewards to the child for good behavior is that he quickly learns to bribe Mother with disturbing behavior in order to get them. Bribery learned in the family is easily generalized to involve the rest of society where the child threatens misbehavior unless he is rewarded.

One example of child-bribing concerns a professional who used pieces of candy to toilet train his oldest child. It worked rather effectively with her and she was trained without too much fuss. However, when this was tried on the second child, the professional experienced some surprising results. The child went to the bathroom, urinated, and was given a piece of candy. The trainer found, however, that the time between bathroom trips became shorter and shorter. In fact, it got so that she would go to the bathroom, urinate, come out, get her candy and then repeat the performance over and over again in quick succession. The child had learned to control the situation to get the maximum number of candies possible. The question arises as to which one is doing the training, the parent or child.

Remember that children are very creative. They have their free agency and are much more active in affecting their environment than we have believed in the past. There are usually better ways of changing misbehavior to more correct or desirable behavior than through issuing of rewards, which have little to do with the actual behavior itself.

Have Enjoyable Times Together

Mother, plan your schedule so that a certain amount of time is set aside each day where you can have fun with your children. This is important because you build a reservoir filled with good relationship experiences, which will help carry you through conflicts. Enjoyable experiences should be carefully planned at times and spontaneous at other times. However, some scheduling for fun should be done; otherwise, busy mothers tend to neglect it in favor of more pressing duties. Positive feelings that are developed during periods of fun will tend to pervade the more routine relationships during the day.

Family Council

The Church has suggested and has gone to great expense, time and effort to encourage the family to hold family home evenings. The primary purpose of this is to teach children the gospel and train them to become good Christians. The family should also hold a family council at this or some other time where family problems can be resolved in a rather democratic way and future planning can occur. This is a time where the children gain experience in becoming responsible, democratic citizens through the parents allowing them the right to be involved in making of decisions regarding their welfare and that of the whole family. This does not mean that children of all ages should be involved in all decision-making in the family. However, there are always areas where even the youngest can be involved in experiencing the responsibility of making decisions within a group. If Mother encourages some decision-making when the child is very young, she will be able to gradually increase the boundaries wherein the child can make decisions as he grows older.

Allowing children the right to make decisions and the right to be involved in decision-making within the family council is one of the most difficult problems for many families. The reason for this is that too often mothers and fathers dictatorily impose their own wishes on the family without allowing the children the right to express their feelings. Parents become used to this kind of relationship; subsequently, when they try to implement a more democratic system, they become threatened and are afraid they will lose control and that their children will behave irresponsibly.

However, when children are given the right to participate in making decisions, especially when they are very young and grow up with the experience of making decisions, it is surprising how very responsibly they do behave.

A distinct advantage to the family council is that children identify with the family and feel that they have a part in its functioning and movement. One of the problems in society today is alienated youth. One probable reason for their alienation is that they were not given the opportunity of becoming responsibly involved in decision-making processes in the family.

Guidelines for a Family Council

1. Meet regularly at scheduled periods, for example, seven o'clock each Thursday night.
2. Each member of the family participates in the decision-making processes as much as his psychological, emotional and social development will allow.
3. Remember that the family council is a learning experience and many errors will be made.
4. Father presides, but each member takes turns in conducting, even the youngest, if possible.
5. Family members are not required or forced into attending. They will learn it is for their own best interests to participate when decisions are made by the family which influence them.
6. Each member of the family is free to express his feelings and ideas. Ideas should be offered for consideration, not imposed.
7. The approach is positive, not negative. As soon as a problem is presented, constructive ideas are voiced. The family council is not allowed to degenerate into a gripe session.
8. Parents allow the children to experience the results of their decisions. Each family member gets one vote and it is only when the decision made is dangerous that parents exercise their veto right. Some

pain is beneficial for learning. The majority should learn to live with their poor decisions until the next scheduled family council meeting.

9. The family council is the chief authority for the family. It is through active participation in what happens to them that children learn to use their God-given free agency in responsible ways. Parents are cautioned to let their children have the freedom and responsibility to learn responsible citizenship by not stepping in and protecting them from their poor decisions.

10. Have faith and trust in your children that they will learn to behave responsibly in the family council and they will not disappoint you. Expect some problems in getting started, especially if your children are older. Often they are surprised with their new-found responsibility and may be somewhat suspicious. They may test you to see if you are really going to include them in the decision-making process. Stick with it. The beginning is hardest.

11. Start with one, a few, then more areas for their consideration when your children are not used to participating in family decisions. The early unloading of too many areas for decisions can swamp the inexperienced family council. Areas for family decisions can be enlarged as the family gains experience and training.

Summary

This chapter has reviewed some principles that have been effective in attaining the Christian and democratic objectives discussed in Chapter I. These principles do not exhaust all possible situations; however, they are sufficient to give mothers a sound basis for dealing with their children.

Chapter VI is concerned in more detail with misbehavior and how to handle it. The principles discussed in the present chapter are there applied to specific situations.

REFERENCES

Beier, Ernst G. *The Silent Language of Psychotherapy.* Chicago: Aldine Publishing Company, 1966.

Christensen, Oscar C. and Raymond Lowe. Information gained by the author in counseling sessions at the Parent Teacher Education Center, University of Oregon, 1964-1966.

Dreikurs, Rudolph, et al. *Adlerian Family Counseling: A Manual for Counseling Centers.* Eugene: University of Oregon Press, 1959.

Dreikurs, Rudolph. *ABC's of Guiding the Child.* A class handout at the University of Oregon, November of 1961.

Dreikurs, Rudolph. *Challenge of Parenthood.* New York: Duell, Sloan and Pearce, 1958.

Dreikurs, Rudolph. *Psychology in the Classroom, A Manual for Teachers.* New York: Harper and Row, Publishers, 1957.

Dreikurs, Rudolph, and Vicki Solz. *Your Child and Discipline.* Washington: The National Education Association, Publishers, No. 382-11708.

Lowe, Raymond. "Some Principles for Living with Children," An Unpublished Class Handout at the University of Oregon.

CHAPTER V.

Applying the Principles

Introduction

Mother should train her child when the atmosphere is calm and peaceful between them, when there is a good relationship. This suggests planning and purposeful action rather than emotional reactions to crises and problem situations. The more Mother works at training the child, the fewer will be her problems with him.

Recent experiments with newborn babies and young children indicate that they are much more intelligent and capable of learning than was previously believed. The young child is very creative and appears to be very much aware of his environment. The child has great resilience. He is not fragile. He has great resources of strength from which to draw. Apparently, for most children, the effects of heredity are minimal. The implications are that the training the child receives when very young is of prime importance in preparing him for life.

Principles of Learning

An exhaustive review of learning principles is not to be attempted in this section; however, a few of the major ones are discussed. It should be remembered that underlying all learning is the basic striving of the child to have a secure place of belonging with those important to him. Mother and Father are usually the most important people in the child's life.

A few learning principles on which Mother can base the training of her child include:

1. The child tends to learn and repeat those things which bring about results that are perceived by the child as pay off. Usually, pay off is viewed by him

in relation to his place of belonging with those important to him in the family, i.e., Mother and Father.

2. The child learns through imitation by observing and mimicking significant other people in his life. Mother is usually a first model used by the child for this kind of learning. He observes the consequences of Mother's behavior, and, if he perceives the pay off as meeting his desired goals, he will tend to imitate her. The child may also imitate the behavior of Mother or copy her in order to get closer and identify more with her. Anthropologists are very much aware of this kind of learning.

3. The child needs successful experiences in learning if he is to have the courage to continue to learn. Some experiments indicate that the typical child should experience at least three success experiences to one failure.

4. Each child is different and will develop or learn at his individual rate depending on the environment and the learning which the child has already experienced.

5. For successful learning to take place, the learner must have desire within himself to learn. He must be motivated.

6. The tasks or concepts to be learned should not be too hard or too easy for best learning to occur.

7. Fresh, novel, and stimulating experiences tend to encourage the child to learn.

8. Active participation by the child stimulates him and encourages the learning process.

9. Discipline that is coercive and overly strict produces rigid conformity, anxiety, shyness or aggression and deference to authority figures. The learning process becomes threatening for the child.

10. Criticism increases failure and discouragement. It tends to lower the child's self-confidence and his level of aspiration.

11. Learning, which cannot be forced or commanded, comes from within the child.

12. The most rapid learning occurs during infancy and early childhood; therefore, Mother is in a key position.

13. It is generally better to distribute training over a period of time.

14. Some research indicates that the single most important attribute of any teacher for stimulating learning is that of friendliness.

During the past several decades there has been great emphasis on maturation and readiness to learn. This generally has been put in a context of physical growth and development; however, recent studies indicate that it is not so much a physical readiness to learn as it is that the "ready" child has learned those things that are necessary for further learning to take place. There is some reason to believe, then, that the child can learn to learn and that those involved in teaching him, whether it be Mother or a public school teacher, can help him to learn by providing him with those experiences basic to additional learning. The implications of the new research is that developmental tasks and stages of maturation have been possibly overemphasized. The emphasis in the future should be on helping the child to learn to learn.

Mother as a Teacher

As suggested previously, some research indicates that a very important characteristic in the child's learning environment are the personality traits of the teacher. Mother should be aware of those things about her personality which tend to be conducive to his learning new things and those which tend to discourage.

Personality traits of Mother that tend to *discourage* learning are:

1. abruptness
2. coldness

3. a quick temper —
4. aloofness
5. acting high and mighty
6. being "preachy" —

In contrast, it seems that a good mother-teacher *encourages* learning when she is:

1. warm —
2. easy going —
3. relaxed, having a friendly manner
4. simple and approachable
5. having a good sense of humor
6. showing a ready smile —
7. well-organized —
8. confident
9. able to set limits
10. consistent
11. flexible
12. curious about the world and having an urge to explore and find out things
13. able to communicate well. —

Mothers who are calm, casual, and maintain routine and order, tend to raise peaceful, calm and serene children who develop into courageous learners.

There are many problems besetting Mother as she attempts to train her child. One of these is that of wanting to prove to other people that she is a "good mother." Often this gets in the way of mothers being just that. So called "good mothers" tend to give in to the pressures of others. This is especially true when others are relatives.

Another problem is the mother who is basically anxious and unsure of herself. She tends to indulge, spoil, and pamper the child. He quickly learns to read the unsureness in his mother's behavior and uses various pressures to manipulate her to get his own way. He may cry, act helpless, or bully her. He may even manipulate relatives and neighbors to bring pressure on Mother to give into his demands. Mother needs to learn the difference between actual needs of the child and devices which he uses to keep her uselessly or destructively involved with him.

Establishing Identity and Worth as a Person

One of the most tragic experiences a person can face is to grow as an adult, not knowing who he is. Psychologists are continually faced with people who do not have an identity of their own, and are uncertain of their own value. A little child is quite unsure of who he is, what he looks like, and how he fits into the world. It is Mother's obligation to train him to have a more incisive self-definition, greater confidence in himself, and greater self-esteem. The child becomes himself as he discovers his world, including himself.

There are many concrete things which Mother can do to help the child to establish his own identity and worth as an individual. One of the best ways is to use his name rather than the belittling, "Hey there!" or a nonrecognizing "Come here." Another effective technique is to have him stand in front of a mirror and discuss with him the image that is reflected back. Also, the use of snapshots is a very effective device. The Polaroid camera is especially useful, for it provides a picture in a matter of seconds. This gives an immediate return to the child. Mother's look, touch, and word reflect to the child her feelings about him which he tends to define and redefine as his feelings about himself. Mother's use of descriptive songs about the child helps him in discovering himself. Another method is to have him lie on a large piece of paper and draw his outline. It may also be helpful to talk about things that belong to the child by saying such things as "This is Johnny's bear," or "These are Johnny's shoes." Another useful procedure is to provide situations so the child can develop his talents. The child discovers himself as he sees what he can do with clay, paint, blocks and etc.

The child can be helped to evaluate himself as a worthwhile person by having his achievements and efforts accepted by Mother. Her praise and admiration can be given freely for his accomplishments. Use such phrases as "What a high jumper you are, John," "Johnny has built a car out of blocks that looks just like a real car," "You waited very patiently, Johnny, for Mother to put the food on the table." If Mother truly admires his efforts and accomplishments the child learns to think of himself as being unique and worthwhile.

Mother should not praise the child or give admiration for his good looks or cuteness, as this encourages the child to vanity and pride.

It is also important that Mother help the child to become aware of his feelings. This can be accomplished in part by Mother asking him how a particular situation or a person made him feel. Mother then accepts whatever feelings the child expresses. This enables the child to become aware that he is a person with feelings. As he identifies these feelings he will be helped to identify himself as an individual entity. Mother's helping the child to learn that he has certain rights by respecting them herself will also assist him to establish his own identity.

In summary, it is suggested that the child can establish his own identity and develop a feeling that he is worthwhile if he has the above experiences with Mother. Mother's respect of the child and her approval of him assist him in this quest.

Training for Motor Control and Coordination

"Motor control" is the ability of the child to use the large and small muscles of his body to achieve his objectives. Such things as walking, running, controlling bowels and bladder, eating whole foods and using fine muscles are included.

Walking

Children begin walking about as early as eight months and as late as about fourteen months. As the child learns to walk there is opportunity to teach him courage and self-reliance. Mother should arrange the room in such a manner

that the child can walk from chair to chair or couch to
chair on his own. These are arranged so that when he falls
he can pick himself up and continue to walk. It encourages
the child to take short steps on his own rather than relying
on Mother. The objects should be gradually separated as
the child gains skill in walking.

A problem for the child who is learning to walk is the
over anxious mother who runs to him and "babys" him when
he falls. This is discouraging to him, for the action communicates "You must be careful or you will get hurt,"
"There is danger in learning how to walk, and adults must
help you." It is much more encouraging for Mother to
stay where she is and calmly say such phrases as, "I am
sure you can make it," "Attaboy!" "Try again," or "Hey,
you're getting better." Mother should not hover over the
child as he learns to walk. It is best to give the child space
and leave him alone. Let him explore and experiment by
himself.

Play

Play is the vocation of the child. It is his important
school and business. Through play the child discovers himself, his body, its functions, and how to use it. He also
discovers how to explore and manipulate the objects about
him. It is through play that development takes place and
self-reliance is encouraged. The child is dependent upon
play for his progress. Adults observing children at play
too often criticize it as a waste of time. This is in error.
Mother should structure the environment so the child has
plenty of opportunity and time to play. Only occasionally
should she get involved with the child's playing as it is
easily used by her to fulfill her needs rather than those of
the child. He should have plenty of time for unstructured
free play alone and with children his own age.

Toilet Training

There is a tendency, especially among middle - class
Americans, to pressure children to become toilet trained

at a very early age. Some have attempted to train their children by the time they are ten months of age. This often results in difficulties for the child and problems in the relationship between the child and his mother. The child should not be toilet trained in a forced, unnatural way. The muscles of the child have to develop before he is able to control his waste elimination.

When the child is about eighteen months, he can usually be toilet trained. Mother should approach this task in a consistent and orderly way. Routine is the key to good toilet training. It is suggested that about every two hours the child be placed on the "potty." Praise him and talk to him when he does eliminate.

As the child learns to use the "potty," he will occasionally revert to eliminating in diapers or on the floor. When he does this, he should not be scolded nor should attention be drawn to it in any way. Mother should re-emphasize the routine of taking the child, every two or three hours, to the "potty."

Mother should remember that progress in toilet training, as in all learning, does not occur as steady and consistent improvement. There will be lapses. When Mother allows herself to get involved with the child in scolding or ridiculing him for his imperfections in toilet training, she is putting herself in the position of being vulnerable to his manipulations, for he learns that he can use waste elimination to keep her busy with him or as a device for defeating her.

The keys to good toilet training are routine and a calm, casual, and patient mother.

The more Mother can encourage the child to take care of himself in areas such as dressing, eating, getting up, doing chores around the house, tidiness, and in toilet training, the more the child will be stimulated to strive for independence.

Accidents During Training

Life is full of accidents. This is especially true of the child as he learns to handle himself and deal with his environment. It is important that the child be taught to have the courage to keep trying even though he experiences difficulty or failure. During these early years, much can be done to help the child to have a courageous outlook on life by teaching him to increase his efforts in the face of accidents. Mother's faith and example are quickly adopted by the child as his own. When accidents occur, Mother's calm courage and the use of phrases such as, "It's OK," "Keep trying, it will come," will do much to build a courageous personality. If Mother is anxious and fearful she will tend to raise a fearful and anxious child. Fear, timidity, and anxiety tend to result in more accidents for the child. If the child develops a courageous stance toward life in his early, formative years, he will tend to be a courageous adult.

Training for Living with Others

Possibly this is the area handled least well by most parents and our educational institutions. It is ironic that our society has produced such an abundance of material wealth and yet so few people able to get along well with others. The family is the first and generally the most important institution for the development and training of skills in social living. If children are competitive, hostile and angry one with another and see others as a threat to their finding acceptance with Mother, they tend to respond similarly as adults. In contrast, the child tends, as an adult, to respond cooperatively if Mother provides an environment where he feels he has a secure place with her. His place is not threatened by the other brothers and sisters.

Mother can work toward training the child to gain skills in social living by providing him with experience in playing and working alone and cooperatively with other children. He should also have experience in sharing, taking turns with other children while maintaining his own rights to property. Mother can provide experience for the child in taking and sharing responsibility in the planning of games as well as in their playing. The child should gain experience in establishing and evaluating standards for living together, in evaluating work, and in observing and being aware of limits set by others. The family council is an excellent vehicle for this. Groups with which the child should have experience for his social skills development include the family, the child's own age group, and other adults.

If Mother expects the child to be courteous with others, it is imperative she be courteous with him. The child will tend to imitate Mother. One error which some make is that of discourteously forcing their own conversation and will on their children. One good rule to follow is to talk to the child when he talks to you or when he seems to need association; otherwise leave him alone. This respects his right to privacy. By respecting his privacy rights you will also be teaching him respect for other peoples' right to privacy.

Comparing the child's behavior or performance to that of other children is very discouraging in developing within the child a desire to interact constructively with others. Mother should not compare the child with others. It stimulates competition and the idea of vertical relationships among people. The child who is compared will tend to feel he lives in a world of superiors and inferiors and that his place is only secure as long as he is able to put others down. This is disastrous for constructive social living and it is at the root, the author believes, of the quarrels and wars of today.

In summary, when Mother is non-comparing, trusting, interested in people, and genuinely interested in what the child does, he will tend to be encouraged to relate to people in cooperative, constructive ways. The relationship Mother establishes with the child tends to be the model which he uses as he interacts with others. If the interaction is cooperative and respectful, he is encouraged to establish orderly, cooperative, and friendly relationships with others. Social skills are developed through encouraging the child to (1) take turns, (2) share, (3) grow in understanding that others have certain rights, and (4) increase his ability to constructively contribute to the welfare of the group and the individual needs of others.

Training to Communicate

There are many ways in which the child can communicate. Earliest of course, the child learns to cry, smile, and laugh. He learns to communicate through body movements and then through the use of words. He communicates using words, phrases, and then sentences.

Mother can do many things to encourage the child in his ability to communicate. Possibly most important is the establishment of a secure relationship with the child. He learns to talk effectively by being listened to and responded to in a secure relationship by a person who cares about him.

There are many techniques that Mother can use to facilitate the language development of her child. She should speak very clearly and distinctly in order to be a good model for the child to follow. Often children who speak poorly are found to have poor adult models. Mother should always use simple and direct language with the child. Playing with him with the simple word games is also very effective. Talking with him about the stories in his books stimulates his language development. The wise mother will use much conversation in interacting with the child, and in reflecting the world to him. As Mother works around the house, she should talk to him about what she is doing. It also stimulates thinking and talking using words showing relationships such as "big-little," "light-heavy," "red-white," "long-short," and etc. Mother's singing to him can stimulate the child's language development.

It is helpful when working directly with the child on his language skills to break larger words up into syllables for him to imitate and master. When a child has trouble with such words as "yellow" (lellow), it is helpful to play a game with him by having him speak a series of easier words starting with "y" (yes, yard, yippy, etc.). The hard word can then be put at the end of the series and the child will quickly get the idea. When he does get closer to the correct pronunciation, Mother's use of such phrases as an excited "John, you're getting closer," will tend to reinforce the learning.

One of the best methods in encouraging children to speak clearly is to fail to understand when they speak poorly. The author is reminded of a five-year old boy who, it was assumed, could not learn how to talk. He used only gestures, grunts, and groans to get those things he needed. It was suggested to Mother that she not see his gestures nor hear his grunts and groans. She was told to pay attention only when he talked. The child soon pointed to the water faucet and grunted, indicating that he wanted a drink of water. Mother's routine reaction would have been to respond by giving him the drink. This time she did not. She refused to pay any attention. The child kept pointing, grunting and groaning; however, Mother refused to hear or see him. This went on for some time, and finally the child stamped his foot and said, "Darn it, I want a drink of water."

The mother who is sensitive to the child's every mood cue discourages him from talking. He gets what he wants without having to learn how to develop the spoken language. Mother should soon insist that the child ask verbally for those things he wants. A "deaf mother" can be a great assistance to the language development of her child.

Another danger of Mother's sensitivity to the physical and "non-language" vocal cues used by the child is that many children find a special unique place with Mother, using such cues. The child develops a special society between himself and his mother. This is a big payoff for not using language. Having a special, private relationship discourages and inhibits the child in developing skill in language communication.

The mother who "baby talks" with her child inhibits his language development. Baby talk is considered cute by many adults; however, the child quickly learns to use it as a technique for keeping Mother busy and involved with him. This hinders learning.

Another thing that tends to inhibit language development of the child is the critical mother who scolds and ridicules the halting attempts of the child as he practices. Such phrases as, "I can't hear you," "You'll just have to learn to pronounce your words more carefully," are inhibiting. Also, laughing at the child as he makes mistakes or being too busy to listen to him are actions that are discouraging.

Mother should encourage the child to express himself not only through words, but through his molding and painting of objects by using clay and paints. Cutting out varying shapes with scissors stimulates communication. Encouraging the child to move his body to the moods and rhythms of music contributes to helping him develop his communication skills. Anything Mother can do to stimulate the free expression of the child tends to stimulate the child's communication and language development.

Playmates

The child's early association with other children his own age is important for his social development. He must have the experience of interacting with his peers. It is imperative that Mother encourage this by structuring the environment so that it is possible. The child should have some contract with children his own age about the time he is walking. The amount of contact should be gradually increased as he gets older. Learning to relate to brothers and sisters and neighborhood children can be helpful.

The child may hestitate about leaving the safety of his mother and use all kinds of techniques in order to manipulate Mother to keep him close to her. He may cry and whimper in order to get Mother to sympathize and take pity on him, or he may use temper tantrums. He may show bruises to encourage Mother to believe that other kids are picking on him and that he cannot get along by himself with them. An anxious mother often feeds into the child's goals of getting her to give special service and protection by keeping him by her side. Mother should realize what the child is feeling, but she should be gentle and firm with him. It may encourage the child to use such phrases as, "I know you can work it out with them. I know how you feel, but you can learn." This is to be done in a quiet voice, which communicates to the child that you have confidence in his ability to work through his social problems.

It is imperative that Mother stay out of the squabbles and situations that a child has with his playmates; otherwise, the child quickly learns to manipulate Mother to protect him. This discourages the child from learning to work things through with others in conflict situations, for he relies on Mother to resolve things for him. If he is not encouraged to handle conflicts, he becomes a discouraged person who has low self-esteem and very little confidence in himself. He becomes an adult who runs to his boss when he has problems with his co-workers.

An indirect way in which Mother can help the child to have the courage, strength and insight to get along with other people is to encourage the child to learn about himself. Once the child truly learns to understand his own feelings, emotions, desires, difficulties and strengths, he will learn to better understand other people and how to get along with them.

Sharing

Most children go through periods when it is difficult for them to share their things with others. One reason for this is that they learn to experience a feeling of owning, which is an important part of their development. Most mothers, due to real or imagined pressures from other adults, force sharing. Mother means well in such situations; however, she is too often overconcerned with her own prestige rather than being aware of the needs of the child. The child must first have a real feeling that what he has is his own before he can truly share. Sharing can be forced on the child, but this is usually ineffective.

Some guidelines to help train your child to share are:
1. Respect the child. Let him have the right to genuine ownership. This is important and is crucial to his security and general development.

2. When another child wants the toy with which your child is playing, and he refuses to share, say nothing and do nothing at this time. Do not pressure the child in front of others to share. Do not get involved.
3. Give him an example by sharing with him things that you have.
4. Talk to the child about sharing at times other than when he is emotionally involved in claiming his own.
5. Have faith in the child that he can and will learn to share.

Chores Around the House

When Mother encourages the child's active participation in doing household chores, she encourages the child to identify with the well-being of the family as well as teaching him independence and self-confidence. It also encourages the child to cooperate for the welfare of others. Little children are eager to do their part to help. Too often Mother, rather than being bothered with the child, will not allow him to help. The message that is given to the child is, "You're not good enough. Mom can't be bothered with you." This is discouraging, and if it continues the child is soon unwilling to help. A child, even at the age of three, can learn to dry dishes. He can be given spoons and plastic utensils to dry. This gives him a sense of accomplishment and feelings of being worthwhile. The very young child should be allowed to help. It should not be demanded.

Guidelines which Mother can follow as she helps a little child to contribute to the upkeep of the house are:
1. do not criticize
2. do not set your standards too high or expect perfection
3. never punish
4. work alongside the child
5. praise him for his efforts and/or accomplishments

The child needs to feel that he is contributing something worthwhile. Many subsequent problems can be averted if Mother will take the time when he is young to encourage cooperative contributions.

As the child gets older he may refuse to do his chores. When this happens an excellent training technique whereby he can learn the logical consequences of uncooperative behavior is for Mother to demonstrate that cooperative living together is a "two way street." If the child refuses to help around the house it is reasonable for Mother to refuse to do so much for him. She may say to the child, "John, if you will no longer sweep off the walks, I will have to do it. Therefore, I will no longer have time to iron your clothes." Such behavior by Mother will help him learn that he must give to others if he expects others to give to him.

Stimulate Independence

Something that Mother should remember is that each child has the need and the right to do for himself whatever he is able to do. Another way of saying this is *do not do for the child what he can do for himself*. A common mistake of the mother who is overly concerned about being a "good mother" is the tendency to want to do everything for the child. The message that is communicated to him when Mother does too much is "You are weak. You are incompetent. Let Mother, who is more efficient, do it for you." This is most discouraging.

Mother should strive to encourage the child as soon as possible to take responsibility for his own dressing, undressing, feeding, putting away of toys and use of the toilet. When the child discovers himself as a more independent person he will feel more worthwhile and confident. This is important for his sense of well-being as a child and later as an adult. The pampered child who is able to manipulate Mother to do things for him that he can do for himself grows up as an insecure adult who feels inadequate, incompetent, and worthless. Mother should encourage the child to use his body and mind for increasing independence, which will stimulate in the child self-respect and the confidence that he can handle his environment.

Dressing

About the age of two or three the child should be dressing himself. It can be an enjoyable experience, a time of play, for the child. When he dresses himself he is learning to be self-reliant and to take pride in his ability to do things. Words that point to his accomplishments tend to encourage him. Expressions such as, "Johnny, you've put your shirt on." "Johnny, you are able to put your shoes on," spoken in a tone of voice that indicates you are proud of his ability to grow and develop will contribute much to his self-confidence. The child will refuse to let you help him dress as he develops pride in his new found achievements.

When he is dressing, Mother should not demand that he dress himself nor put him under pressure and compulsion to do this. It should be something that is natural for him and something that he takes pride in doing. Mother's pride in Johnny's accomplishment will encourage him.

If Mother is having difficulty with the child, dressing can be a battleground between the two. We often find the child will demand service from Mother in order to keep her busy with him. One excellent way he has of doing this is through getting Mother to dress him. The child may act helpless or do things wrong expressly for the purpose of getting Mother involved. The child who is unsure of his place with Mother in relation to the other children, often uses getting Mother to dress him as a technique to get special consideration at the expense of the other children. An example of this is a five-year old boy who came down every morning to breakfast with his shoes on the wrong feet. He would stand in front of Mother, staying in her way until she noticed his shoes. Mother repeatedly told him to change them. He ignored her. Mother would then stop all she was doing, sit him down and place the shoes on the right feet. The counselor asked if the shoes were on the wrong feet every morning, and Mother said, "Yes, indeed they are." The counselor then asked if she knew why this occurred, and Mother said, "Well, it is just because Johnny does not know which shoe goes on which foot." The counselor proposed that if that were the case the laws of probability would dictate that some mornings he would have his shoes on the correct feet. Mother's jaw dropped in surprise at her new awareness of what the child was doing. He was the youngest in the family. It was his way of being noticed and of causing Mother to devote her attention to him alone.

In summary, Mother should commend her child for his ability in getting himself dressed. She should not expect him to be dressed as well as he would if she were to dress him. She should also beware not to feed into the special demands of the child who uses dressing as a game to keep Mother busy and involved with him.

Eating

Demanding that the child eat is a special trap. Anxious mothers tend to become demanding and coercive at mealtime. Meals become a battleground with "good mothers" demanding that their children eat in large quantities, or insisting they have some of everything on their plates so they will have a good diet. This encourages conflict between mothers and their children.

Mealtime is a place where children can more easily outmaneuver their mothers. It is a time for getting special attention or a time for defeating Mother in power struggles. The mother who spoon feeds her child when he can feed himself is giving special service. Also, if a child refuses to eat at Mother's insistent demands, he defeats her and achieves his goal of being boss.

Mealtime has potential for further cementing good relationships among members of the family if it is handled correctly. It is one of the few times during the day family members are together. It should be a pleasant, orderly, and successful experience for the whole family. Pleasant conversation should exist at the table and the emotional atmosphere should be warm and devoid of stress.

Following are some guidelines for encouraging the child's eating habits and improving the efficacy of mealtime:

1. As long as the child is too young to feed himself, he is a distraction and should eat at another time.

2. Eating at the table with others should be a privilege, not a right.

3. Mealtime should be a relaxed period, free of emotional stress.

4. If the child is playing hard, call him early to give him the opportunity of quieting down before he eats.

5. Serve small portions. It is much better that he ask for seconds than be discouraged by large first servings.

6. Usually the child will decide for himself how much food he actually needs. Generally, the larger child will eat more than the smaller one and the active will eat more than the less active.

7. Do not force the child to eat a given amount of food.

8. Use dishes that will not tip or break easily. Dishes that tip and break are discouraging to the child.

9. The food should be easy to get into the mouth and chew.

10. The child will spill and have other accidents at the table. Do not get upset by them. Respond with a calm voice.

11. Introduce new foods in very small amounts and do not demand that the child eat them. Often a new food will be accepted if it is combined with a food that is preferred.

12. The child's appetite will vary from time to time just as adults' appetites vary. Do not expect him to eat the same amount of food each time.

13. Often the child will prefer bland food such as rice and macaroni.

14. You can help the child to develop new understandings through talking about how new foods taste, feel, look, and are colored.

15. Allow the child some freedom to choose his own food. This will encourage his decision-making ability and his feeling that he has some say in what he eats.

16. The physical atmosphere will have an influence on the child's attitude towards eating. Usually a bright, well-ventilated, and clean room and a table set with attractive plates, cups and eating utensils that can be easily managed by the child stimulate the child to eat.

17. There should be an orderly pattern for meals. Specified times for eating should be scheduled. Just as playtime, nap time, and bath time are helpful to the emotional and physical well-being of the child, so are scheduled mealtimes.

18. If the child insists on being disruptive, he should be given a choice of either quieting down or leaving the table. He does not have the right to infringe on the rights of others.

19. It is best that Mother allow the child to miss the meal if he sets a pattern of coming late.

20. If the child dawdles with his food and keeps others waiting on him, Mother quietly removes the plate along with the others and scrapes the remains down the garbage disposal. This should be done with no conversation. Often a child who eats slowly is using it as an attention-getting mechanism to get Mother to nag and become involved with him.

When Mother becomes overly concerned about the child and his eating habits, she is making herself more vulnerable to his manipulations. For the manipulative child, eating becomes a game to keep Mother busy with him.

The less concerned Mother is with a child's eating the proper amount and the right kinds of foods, the more nature will work for her through the natural hunger of the child and the more he will enjoy eating.

Getting Up

Getting the child up in the morning is sometimes a very difficult chore. We often find mothers who make a habit of calling their children six or seven times. They keep going back and forth, finally drag the children out and take them to school for fear they will be late. This, again, is the child's way of getting Mother involved with him and getting her to give him special service. The child feels very important when he is able to get Mother to call five or six times, to help dress him when he is late, and then — this is the final victory — get her to drive him to school.

Mother should get an alarm clock for the child and have him take the responsibility of getting up in the morning. If an alarm clock is not used, Mother should call once, then let natural consequences take over. If the child does not get up in time for breakfast, he misses breakfast. If he gets up late for school, he takes the consequences of the rules of the school. When Mother is unemotional, firm with her own behavior, and allows the child to face the responsibility of his getting up late, he soon learns to accept the responsibility himself.

It is sometimes difficult for the mother who feels, "What will the school officials think of me if Johnny isn't there on time?" or "Johnny just can't go without his breakfast because he will be sick if he doesn't eat." These feelings play into the hands of the manipulative child. If Mother is concerned about what the school teacher will think, she might contact the teacher and inform her of what she is training the child to do. This helps to desensitize Mother and she will tend to have the courage to be more firm with the child.

Remember, Mother, any time you want something more for the child than he wants for himself, you are putting yourself in the position of being more vulnerable to his manipulations.

Tidiness

In tidiness as in many other things, Mother can set the example by being tidy herself. This does not mean a rigid tidiness that becomes a ritual, but rather a tidiness that improves order and ease in living. Mother should be a model who cooperatively works with the child as she trains him to be tidy.

It is important that Mother arrange things to encourage self-reliance on the part of the child. For example, the child can have a special place to hang his clothes by himself without having to rely on an adult. The placing of a clothes closet rod within his reach will accomplish this. His toothbrush should be where he can reach it. Also, his bed should be placed conveniently so that he can more easily learn how to make it.

There should be a place for storing toys. Many children leave their toys out for Mother to stumble over and put away. If he insists on leaving his toys out after he is finished playing with them, Mother should pick them up and put them away out of the child's reach. She then tells him that as soon as he can agree to put his toys back in their proper place when he is through playing with them, he can have them back. The child is given only those toys he puts back in place. Other toys are added as he demonstrates he will put them away.

Mother should not set expectation and standard levels which one would expect of an adult. She should remember the child is learning. Mother should beware of perfectionism and expect error to occur as he learns.

By noticing improvement in the child and by praising him and pointing out his improvements, Mother will encourage the child to further growth in responsible behavior.

Guiding the Child to Self-Discipline

One of the basic requirements for the child in developing self-discipline is for Mother to provide an orderly world in which the child can function within set limits. The child is rather amoral. It is through warm and consistent relationships with adults and positive experiences with authority figures that the child learns to accept limits and begins to understand such concepts as right and wrong. His relationships with significant adults, especially with Mother, lay a foundation for much of his active conscience. It is important that Mother train the child to accept the consequences for what he does. As a child learns to evaluate the consequences of his behavior, he learns to make judgments as to those kinds of behaviors which are constructive and right or destructive and wrong. Mother's basic trust and faith in the child encourage him to have trust and faith in himself which encourage discipline from within.

The child tends to learn self-discipline by having faith in himself, experiencing warm, friendly relations with others, being allowed to experience the consequences of his own behavior, and having much experience in decision making.

Sex Role Education

The child should be encouraged to accept sex both intellectually and emotionally. This includes the acceptance of his own sexual role, i.e., the maleness of the male and the femaleness of the female.

One of the problems in some families is that parents teach their children subtly or directly that males are superior to females. There is possibly a special danger to some males because of common misconceptions concerning the role of the priesthood in the home. Some suggest that the patriarch of the home is a superior being to whom all should unquestioningly submit, including Mother.

Much heartache results for the child who is raised in an environment where he perceives his sexual role as being inferior or superior. When the male is taught he is superior, he tends to strive constantly to meet the dominating, aggressive expectations set for him and continually fears displacement by females. The female, by contrast, tends to feel worthless and builds resentment toward males. This makes it difficult for both to relate respectfully and successfully in marriage.

Mother should teach the child that males and females are equal before God, but that each has a special mission. The mission of the female is bearing and rearing children. The male's is being the medium through which spiritual blessings and ordinances come to the family. He performs the priestly rituals. The missions of both females and males are equal in importance.

Male models are necessary for the young male child. Families where there is divorce or death of the father may not provide a male model for the boys from which they can readily pattern their behavior. There is also this lack in school, for most teachers in the first few grades are women. The mother who does not have a husband can partially compensate for this by encouraging her sons to associate with male relatives who provide good models or others in the neighborhood or Church.

Another way that Mother can stimulate her child to accept his sexual role is to have a good relationship with her husband. It is often found that when the husband ridicules, abuses and dominates his wife, male children tend to have a difficult time adopting their male role, for to them it means to ridicule, punish, and hurt others. This many refuse to do and they reject, therefore, the male role.

Females in a family such as the above would have a difficult time accepting their role because to be female would mean to be abused, hurt, looked down upon, and stepped upon. Many will not accept this and, not having another model, become sexually confused.

The reverse is also true. The wife who belittles her husband, dominates him and is sarcastic with him in front of the children, stimulates her daughters to reject the female role. Sons of such a mother have a difficult time identifying with the father because to be a father means to be ridiculed and trampled on. In order to prevent themselves from being hurt as they see their father hurt, they may identify more with Mother and therefore take on her feminine characteristics.

For children to accept their own sexual roles, it is imperative that Mother and Father establish a good, respectful relationship so that their children will want to model their behavior after their same sex parent.

Sex education of the child can be a very challenging and satisfying experience for parents. The child is naturally and freely curious. If Mother does not answer the child's questions, they will be answered by others in dubious surroundings.

The Church has a very healthy attitude toward sex, which can assist Mother as she educates the child. There are, however, vestiges of the old Puritan ideas that sex is sinful *per se* and therefore is not acceptable before God. The Church teaches that sex is a part of the great plan of mortal existence and is acceptable. We believe the original sin was not sexual; therefore, sex under the law is good before God. Lawful sex is not nasty and something to be feared.

Some principles that parents can follow as they attempt to educate their child are as follows:

1. Answers to questions should be literal and plain.
2. Do not look too far beyond the child's simple, direct question. Very often the child will ask, "Where did I come from, Mommy?" and Mother's mind fearfully jumps to copulation. Only give those answers that the child is asking for directly.
3. Be truthful. Talk honestly to the child.
4. There should be modesty in the home, but it should be natural and easy-going.
5. When parents' inhibitions, fears, and anxieties about sex interfere to the extent that they cannot cope

with the education of their child, they can get a well respected adult who communicates well with children to assist them. This might be a close relative or a trusted friend.

6. Mother and Father, be good female and male models who like yourselves and respect each other so that your children will desire to model their sex role behavior after you.

Training to Give and Accept Affection

One of the difficulties of many people being seen by psychologists and counselors is their inability to give and accept affection. Mother is a key figure in the child's learning to handle affection properly. If Mother establishes a close, affectionate relationship with the child, a pattern for his affectionate relationships with other people will tend to be set. The child seeks and wants a warm, stable and secure relationship with Mother. Affection should be mutually expressed between Mother and child.

If Mother has difficulty expressing affection to the child, he will have difficulty expressing affection to Mother and to others. One way Mother can overcome this is to set up a schedule during the day for approaching the child in affectionate ways. Putting her arm around the child, squeezing him to her two or three times a day and talking to him about things in which he is interested, express affection. Mother can also look into his eyes and tell him how much she appreciates what he does during the day to help her out. Mother's encouraging remarks concerning the child's growth and development can express affection, love and respect.

As the child seeks to display love to Mother, he should not be ridiculed nor criticized if he is awkward in his attempts.

There is one danger. Many children occasionally use affection to demand service from Mother. For affection to have the most meaning, Mother should give it to the child when he is not demanding it. It should be a free gift. If the child uses affection to "butter-up" Mother to allow him to behave in such irresponsible ways as getting out of doing his chores in the home, Mother should ignore him while he is doing so.

There are many ways of training your child to give and accept affection. A warm tone of voice, displaying affection for your husband in front of the child, your faith and trust in the child, your respect of his rights, your love given as a free gift with no strings attached — these all encourage the child to learn to give and accept affection.

Stimulate a Belief and a Faith in God

Mother's faith in God should be strong and stable. Her behavior should be in conformance with her stated religious beliefs. This is a foundation for the child's faith in God. The child must also be trained and educated in the beliefs and doctrines of the Gospel. It is the author's firm belief that when the child has a good relationship with parents who love God he will tend to develop a belief in God his Father and will cling to the Church.

The above, however, is not enough if the child is to have a strong faith in God. There is an indirect route which the author feels is vitally important. Mother must train the child to become self-reliant, independent, and respectful of himself. The child who does not learn self-reliance and self-respect seldom has a stable faith in himself, in the world about him which is the handiwork of God, or in God. Unless the child develops independence and love and respect for himself, his faith in God is usually, at best, unstable. People coming for counseling who doubt themselves, tend to doubt their Heavenly Father. They have little faith in anything.

Three steps to encouraging your child to have faith in God are:

1. Be an example yourself. Have a calm, quiet, stable faith in your Heavenly Father.
2. Teach the child the Gospel of Jesus Christ.

3. Educate and train him in such a way that he can have a strong faith in himself, which is a prerequisite leading to a faith in God.

Encourage Curiosity, Initiative, and Creativity

The world is fresh, new, and wonderful to the young child. Mother can either stimulate the child's natural curiosity and creativity or she can inhibit it. Mothers and school teachers too often suppress the child's desire to see and explore.

Mother can encourage curiosity, initiative, and creativity by thinking, watching, and wondering with the child. She can encourage him by trying to see the world through his eyes and by providing a secure environment where the child feels it is safe to guess, gamble, explore, touch, smell, listen, and look. Lively conversation with the child, free of any danger of ridicule or sarcasm, will stimulate him. Mother can encourage these attributes by asking such questions as, "I wonder what would happen if . . ." rather than saying, "It will never work out." Mother can also help the child to question. She can ask, "What does flour feel like to you? What does the sand feel like to you? I wonder how it got that way? I wonder why the dog has four legs! When do you think these seeds will grow into pumpkins? Which seems smaller to you, a dog or a beetle?" It is generally best not to ask the child direct questions because direct questions calling for specific answers tend to inhibit freedom of response. The child has to then try to guess what answer Mother is after. This is also true of questions calling for "yes" or "no" answers.

Some guides that Mother can use to encourage the child to continually grow in curiosity, initiative and creativity are to:
1. Wonder with him.
2. Always refrain from ridicule.
3. Ask wondering questions to which several responses can be given.

4. Think with the child; wonder and watch with him.

5. Provide success experiences for him.

Stimulate an Appreciation for Things Aesthetic

Blessed is the child who learns to appreciate the beauty in the world about him. The mother who stimulates her child's sensitivity by encouraging him to feel, touch, see, taste, and hear at a very early age is doing her child a great service. If Mother helps her child to see the beautiful, he will have a tendency to live a beautiful life. If he sees beauty in the world there will be a tendency to cling to it and preserve it.

Mother can stimulate her child to appreciate the beautiful in life by experiencing with him the beauties of sunsets, flowers, paintings, concerts, and so on. A good relationship between Mother and child should pervade the aesthetic experiences. The good relationship will tend to make the experiences more beautiful and the beautiful experiences will tend to make the relationship more satisfying to both.

Mother should take time to sharpen her own perception of the beautiful in life in order to assist her child to perceive it. The home should be a place of beauty. If Mother takes pride in setting a nice-looking table, in beautiful decorations, and Father takes pride in a well kept and beautiful yard, the child will learn to see the beautiful and appreciate it.

Other Training Areas

Nursing

Regularity and routine are of importance. In the past, mothers have been taught two extreme positions. One is that the child should be fed upon demand. The other that Mother should hold rigidly to a schedule. Feeding on demand may create problems, for it tends to teach the child to expect people to give in to his demands. When this happens the child may become pampered and spoiled. Holding rigidly to a schedule makes Mother a slave to the schedule.

We suggest that Mother set up a nursing schedule that is most beneficial to her and to her child. The advantages of a schedule are:

1. Regularity and order are important parts of social living in a complex society and routine and order in feeding will help the child learn these.

2. Regularity of food intake encourages and is a concomitant of biological order. It seems that growth is encouraged and facilitated by rhythmical processes.

Your feeding schedule should be set up in consultation with your physician. Each child is somewhat different; however, in the average situation the child is nursed about every four hours. The schedule should be maintained for its benefits. It should not tyrannize the family. A few minutes difference one way or another is not going to make a great impact on the child.

It appears that most errors are the result of Mother's anxiousness and underestimation of the resilience of the baby. The most important thing that Mother should realize in nursing the child is that a quiet, calm attitude is most conducive to proper growth and development. The actual physical feeding is of secondary importance within rather broad limits. An anxious, fearful mother is more detrimental to the child's development than changes in the temperature of the child's formula or the quality of the formula itself. Nursing should be a time in which Mother and the child have pleasant experiences together.

It is also suggested that mothers, especially young mothers, resist the encroachments of well-meaning relatives who insist on interfering. The experience of nursing should be between Mother and child. Mothers-in-law and mothers should allow the new mother the opportunity of enjoying her baby. Their responsibility should be to respect the young mother enough to allow her to be responsible for him. They should not take over nor should they be critical. If help is desired by the new mother, it should be given at a time other than when the baby is being nursed.

In summary, Mother's basic attitude of being calm, quiet, and casual is more important to the child than any slight change in his formula. Well-meaning relatives should not come between Mother and her child. If help is requested, it should not be used by relatives as a means of taking over. Nursing should be a special time between Mother and baby. It should be the start of a good relationship between the two.

Weaning

Weaning the child is one of the most difficult tasks for the "good mother." It is difficult to be firm when the child cries and pouts because he is not getting his bottle any longer. In weaning, as with nursing and many other aspects of the child's life, Mother should set up a routine and stick to it regardless of the angry protests of the child. It is recommended, when the child is to be weaned, that Mother either store the bottles away or put them in the garbage so she will not be tempted to give in to his demands.

One of the problems in weaning is that the child uses manipulative devices, such as crying, whining, pulling a long face, and so on, in order to get Mother to give in to his wants. The child often puts additional pressure on Mother to give him back the bottle when there is a younger nursing child in the family. The older child's goal is to get service just like the younger.

Mother should not give in to the pressure of the child. She can let the child's hunger work for her. A plate is set for the child and it is assumed he will eat. If he does not, Mother does not say anything. She simply picks up his plate and scrapes the food into the garbage disposal. The child is not allowed to eat until the next meal. It is important that Mother be firm with herself and to beware of her own anxieties for the welfare of the child. If she pities him, he will interpret it as weakness in her resolve and will redouble his efforts to get Mother to give in.

Another Baby — A New Arrival

It is often quite difficult for a child to adjust to the arrival of a new baby. This is especially true if he is an only child who has experienced much fondling and caressing from both Mother and Father. When Mother's attention and concern are redirected to the baby, the first child feels threatened by the new arrival and he may resort to many manipulative techniques to keep Mother busy with just him. He may act frightened. He may act helpless. He may revert to baby talking, thumb sucking or wetting his pants in order to get special service. All require special attention from Mother and are the child's ways of pulling the attention of Mother back to him.

There are ways Mother can counteract the child's fear that her attention and love are being taken away from him by the new arrival. One way is to help the child identify with the baby as it begins noticeably forming in the womb. If he is about three years of age, he can be helped to understand how the baby is growing in Mother's tummy. This can help him anticipate the baby. The more Mother can allow and encourage the child to help constructively in the feeding, holding, and generally taking care of the baby after it arrives, the easier it will be for him to accept the new one and to feel that he has a responsible place.

Bedtime

Getting the child to bed can be a most difficult chore for it appears that the child is especially adept at this time in keeping Mother involved with him by demanding special service from her. Getting him several drinks of water and taking him to the bathroom causes her to be busy with him. Not going to bed when asked is another method of keeping Mother involved.

Mother should quietly, but firmly, refuse to give the child service or undue attention by not getting him drinks of water or taking him to the bathroom after he is once in bed. The misbehaving child is not to be talked to after he is in bed. If he needs to go to the bathroom, he goes by himself. Mother says nothing. This will make it difficult for the child to keep Mother engaged with him.

Letting the older child experience the consequences of his own behavior can be helpful in getting him to bed. An example of this is the child who stays up late at night. He is only called once to get up. He may choose to sleep in and be late for school. If he is late to school, Mother doesn't come to his rescue. He is allowed to experience the consequences from the teacher or principal of his being late.

If there are several young children in the family who do not accept the responsibility of turning their lights off and going to sleep, they can be given a choice by Mother of having control of their own lights and turning them off on time by themselves, or having Mother turn off the main control switch. This should be handled by Mother with no emotion but with firmness and confidence. She should be careful to avoid getting herself into an angry power-conflict with the children by being firm and saying nothing.

Mother should establish an atmosphere of quiet before bedtime. There should be no TV or stereo blaring as the child attempts to get to sleep. It should be a quiet time, a peaceful time, a time for sleep. The family can decide together in their family council the time that is best for the children to go to bed.

Mother can encourage the child to go to bed by taking ten or fifteen minutes at bedtime to talk to him in a quiet, peaceful way. She may tell a story or talk to him about his day. This, then, becomes a time to which the child looks forward.

Piano Practicing

There are some things that the child will not recognize as having value. One of these may be the development of his talents. If the child were left on his own, he probably would not develop many of his talents having personal and social value. Mother, therefore, may urge him to work at developing them. She should provide him a choice as to what talents he will work on among those valued by the parents. If he decides to develop his musical talents, he may be given the choice of voice, violin, piano, and etc. The child makes the final decisions within the limitations set by his parents.

The degree of competence expected of the child beyond a given point should be his decision. No parent should decide beforehand that the child is going to become a concert pianist or a concert violinist. This decision, because of the tremendous efforts and the exclusion of other activities, should be left up to the child when he comes to that point in his development.

Time for practicing should be cooperatively worked out with the child and others in the family. Mother should insist that the child put in the time required for practicing; however, choice of time should be worked out in cooperation with the other family members.

Mother should not criticize the child's skill when he is practicing. His half-hour or hour of practice time is strictly between himself and his teacher. Practicing should be considered the responsibility of the child. If he does not practice, the logical consequences are that he not be allowed to take part in the pleasures of life which responsible behavior brings about. Just as man cannot enjoy the fruits of his labors until he has accomplished, neither should the child experience the pleasure of play or TV until he is responsible to himself in developing special valued skills which will enable him to feel better towards himself and also enable him to contribute more to society.

When Mother selects a teacher for her child, her first concern should be the teacher's total personality. She should be a person who respects others and has warmth and love for children. The second concern should be her skill.

The Handicapped Child

Mother is usually more vulnerable to the manipulations of her handicapped child. This is especially true if she feels sorry for him, pities him, or feels guilty because of him. The handicapped should be generally treated like any other child. The basic training techniques are the same with the handicapped as with the typical child. Mother must be firm with him and with herself so as to not allow herself to give undue service or attention.

Death of a Child

The death of a child is a traumatic experience for Mother. However, this is often not nearly as traumatic as its effects on the training practices of Mother with the remaining children. It is often found in our family counseling experiences that mothers who have lost a child tend to be over protective of the other. Mother, experiencing the death of one child, immediately pulls in the boundaries of her other children and anxiously cautions them about the dangers of life. This tends to make them discouraged about their ability to cope with life. They also may use Mother's anxiety and fear against her by manipulating her to be overly involved with them.

It is suggested that when Mother experiences the death of one of her children she take special efforts to prevent her overconcern and fears for the safety of the others from interfering with their opportunities to develop self-reliance.

School — How to Prepare the Child

Home is the foundation for the child's development of those special skills, concepts, and habits which enable him to be successful in school. If he is well prepared in the home, school becomes a successful and enjoyable experience. We are not suggesting that Mother teach the child the alphabet, simple arithmetic, and how to read before he enters school. There are other things much more important for Mother to teach. She is not to do the school's job, but she is to prepare the child with those things which will enable him to take full advantage of the opportunities provided in school.

Mother should be concerned with the child's learning to learn. Following are some of the ways she can train the child which will enable him to be well prepared for his learning experiences in school:

1. Motivate the child to find pleasure in learning experiences.
2. Train the child to live within an orderly system.
3. Train the child to speak correctly.
4. Train the child to take care of himself. He should be able to dress, wash, and cross streets by himself.
5. Give the child a feeling of confidence that he can overcome most obstacles by himself without special assistance from others.
6. Train the child to delay gratification of his needs, wishes, and desires and to work for things which are in the future.
7. Mothers, be a basic source of information and ideas. This will help the child to see adults as people who can give assistance and disseminate information and ideas.
8. Stimulate the child to independence. This prepares him for the new school environment. Beware of spoiling, as this is poor preparation.
9. Train the child to take pride in his own achievement, growth, and development.
10. Stimulate the formation of ideas concerning size, shape, color, form, etc.
11. Provide opportunities for the child to experience many things by visits to such places as a zoo, library, fair, the beach, the mountains, etc., where the child can have many different experiences that will give him a good foundation for learning in school.

12. Talk to him about things that you see, hear, and do. This will encourage him to think and perceive the world about him.

13. Let the child see Mother, Father, and the older children enjoying reading from good books, newspapers, and magazines.

14. Rejoice with the child as he achieves and grows.

15. Encourage him to discriminate, to generalize, and to make judgments. This can be stimulated by Mother pointing out to the child similarities and differences in the objects about him. It will encourage the child to become a thinking person.

16. Encourage him to learn to distinguish reality from fantasy. Help him to distinguish the real physical and social world about him from his daydreams, wishes and hopes.

17. Encourage the child to live socially with others in a cooperative fashion. Help him to understand his own feelings and thoughts and also the feelings and thoughts of others.

18. Allow the child to learn by experience.

Mother has many opportunities to teach the child some of the basic ideas and concepts that are important to his functioning adequately in the new learning situation, the school. Housekeeping experiences have good learning opportunities for the child in concept formation. Mother can talk about the shape of her pans, which are long, round, square, narrow, etc. She can also talk with him about the various colors in the house. She can talk with him about objects that are soft and hard, smooth and rough, etc.

These are some of the concepts (ideas) which are basic to the child's functioning adequately in school. These, along with Mother's introducing the child to an orderly world and training him to cooperatively interact with others, provide a good foundation for him to function effectively in school. Also, if the home is a place where he feels secure, cared for, liked, accepted, and successful, he will tend to anticipate the same things at school and will find them.

Homework

It is generally a mistake for Mother to assist the child with his homework. This is especially true if there are problems between Mother and child. Even where the relationship is good, doing homework with him stimulates conflict and frustration. It is usually frustrating for Mother to try to help the child with his homework because his attempts to please you add a new dimension to the problems and increase the possibilities for anxiety and discouragement. Give assistance only rarely. When you think you must work with him, do it only when he asks and be careful to be calm and patient.

Homework is the teacher's responsibility. Mother should not allow it to be shifted to her shoulders. If the teacher insists that Mother help the child, she is showing her inadequacy. However, as in practicing the piano, a study time should be scheduled. Study is to be completed before he participates in "play" activities.

In summary, homework can be an activity where the child can keep Mother busy and involved with him. His not doing the homework or doing it slothfully or inadequately becomes a technique for keeping Mother busy with him. Keeping her busy becomes more important than doing the homework correctly. It is a place where Mother can easily be defeated if the child's goal is to defeat her. The general rule is to refuse to get involved with the child and his homework. If there is any doubt or conflict whatever, do not assist him.

Summary

Mother can train her child to meet the objectives discussed in Chapter I by following the training guides discussed in this chapter. The following is a brief summary of the objectives themselves and how they are achieved.

Love for God

The child develops a love of God by learning about Him through devout parents; however, this is not enough. The child must also have faith in his ability to cope with his environment and respect for himself and for other people. He will then tend to respect and love God.

Respect and Acceptance of Self

The child will learn to respect and accept himself to the degree that Mother has confidence in him and encourages him with the attitude that he can handle his environment adequately. The key is for Mother to have faith and trust in the child and allow him to experience opportunities for growth and development towards mastery of his environment.

Compassion for Mankind

Mother can encourage love of others by respecting the child and insisting upon his respecting her rights. Also, if the child likes himself, he will tend to like others.

Honesty

If the child is to develop honesty, Mother must respect him enough to deal honestly with him. As the child comes to have faith in himself and in his confidence to meet his environment and life situations in general, he will have no need to hide behind a facade of dishonesty.

Reality

The child will tend to see life much like his Mother sees it. The more realistic Mother is in her appraisal of situations, the more realistic the child tends to become. The more faith the child has in his ability to cope with life situations, the more he will be able to see and understand reality as it exists.

Courage to Continually Strive to Grow

If Mother does not criticize the child when he makes mistakes and encourages him to keep trying in spite of failure, he will tend to have faith and courage to continue to progress throughout life. The child should also be taught the principle of repentance and its effect on continued progress.

Self-Reliance

Possibly the best way that Mother can encourage self-reliance is to encourage and provide opportunities for the child to do for himself. Mother should not do those things for the child that the child can do for himself. Encouragement toward self-reliance can also be provided by Mother praising the child for his efforts as well as his accomplishments. She should eliminate criticism.

Efficiency in Solving Problems

When the child is helped to see things more realistically, he is provided with a basis for approaching the difficulties of life in an efficient manner. Mother's basic honesty will also assist the child. If Mother sees him as being a very worthwhile person and he is encouraged to grow in independence and self-reliance, he will be relatively free of self doubt and serious emotional problems. This will free him as he is taught to focus on problems and think of alternatives for action.

Openness

If Mother is open and honest with the child, he will tend to imitate her behavior and be open and honest himself. Mother can also stimulate this by making, to the child, remarks that encourage openness. He can be stimulated if Mother never criticizes or ridicules him. Mother's calm, casual, and friendly attitude in the face of difficulties will encourage openness.

Balance Or Moderation in All Things

Besides being a good model herself there are things that Mother can do to stimulate a child to achieve a balanced life. One is to have a serene attitude about life in general. Another is to encourage the child to have self confidence and a feeling of worth, which will make it unnecessary for him to "ride any particular hobby horse" in life. Mother can also stimulate the child to have many different experiences in life in many areas, such as in nature, religion, music and the arts, politics, hobbies, and other cultures and peoples.

REFERENCES

Bandura, Albert and Richard H. Walters. *Social Learning and Personality Development*. San Francisco: Holt, Rinehart and Winston, Inc., 1965.

Brigham Young University. Personal interview with Richard Allen, Assistant Professor of Languages. February 18, 1968.

"Daily Program I For A Child Development Center," *Project Headstart Pamphlet No. 4*. Washington, D. C.: Office of Economic Opportunity, Publishers.

Dinkmeyer, Don and Rudolph Dreikurs. *Encouraging Children to Learn: The Encouragement Process*. Englewood Cliffs: Prentice-Hall, Inc., 1963.

Dreikurs, Rudoph. *The Challenge of Parenthood*. New York: Duell, Sloan and Pearce, 1958.

Beyer, Evelyn. *Nursery School Settings — Invitation to What?* New York: The National Association for The Education of Young Children, Publishers, 1958.

Gore, Lillian L. & Rose Koury. *Educating Children in Nursery Schools and Kindergartens*. Washington, D.C.: U.S. Government Printing Office, 1964.

Montagu, N. F. Ashley. "Education and Human Relations," An Address before the 1957 National Convention of the American Association of School Administrators, Atlantic City, February 19, 1957.

McDonald, Fredrick J. *Educational Psychology*. San Francisco: Wadsworth Publishing Company, Inc., 1960.

"Nutrition, Better Eating for a Headstart," *Project Headstart No. 3*. Washington, D.C.: Office of Economic Opportunity, Publishers.

The Priesthood and You: A Course of Study for the Melchizedek Priesthood of the Church of Jesus Christ of Latter-day Saints, 1966. Salt Lake City: The Deseret News Press, 1966. Published by the First Presidency of the Church of Jesus Christ of Latter-day Saints.

The Melchizedek Priesthood Lessons 1965. Salt Lake City: The Deseret News Press, 1965. Published by the Council of the Twelve Apostles of the Church of Jesus Christ of Latter-day Saints.

"Unlocking Early Learning's Secrets," *Life,* LXII (March 31, 1967), pp. 40-7.

Watson, Goodwin. "What Do We Know About Learning," *NEA Journal,* LII (March, 1963), 20-22.

CHAPTER VI.

Correcting the Misbehavior

All children misbehave. Mother's reactions to the child when he is misbehaving determine, in large measure, whether or not the misbehavior becomes more deeply imbedded in his behavior repertoire or is discarded in favor of more positive, constructive behavior. The purpose of this chapter is to provide some guidelines and practice for Mother in correcting the misbehavior. Some basic assumptions concerning the misbehaving child are briefly reviewed and are followed by a more detailed discussion of his A B C D Goals and a varied presentation of some specific, disturbing behaviors with suggestions of how best to correct them. The chapter ends with some cautions and a brief discussion of what Mother can expect from the child as she works at correcting his misbehavior.

Basic Assumptions

1. Family members experiencing much difficulty tend to relate to one another in a vertical-competitive fashion. Children in such families push one another down and away from the parents as they scramble for favored positions.

2. Competitive, vertical behavior impedes or prevents the development of cooperative, warm relationships among family members.

3. A child must feel that he securely belongs if he is to behave constructively.

4. The perceptions of the disturbing child may be logical or illogical. The important thing is his subjective view, not the logic of it. Mother must understand his perceptions if she is to best help him.

5. Though the misbehaving child's responses appear irrational to mother, they make sense to him. They fit in with his personal view of things.

6. The misbehaving child is only dimly aware of his goals. *He does not consciously plan or plot to manipulate Mother.*

7. Mother generally responds to her child when he is misbehaving by doing the first thing that comes to mind. This first impulse is usually what the child is manipulating from her and it tends to reinforce his misbehavior.

8. It is important for Mother to learn to be a careful observer so that she can accurately interpret her misbehaving child. She should learn to read the hidden and subtle cues if she is to understand his goals. Guides for observing are given in Chapter VIII.

The A-B-C-D Goals of Misbehavior

Goals of the misbehaving child are shown in Figure 1. Included are the general types of behaviors used by the child to achieve each of the various goals. It should be noticed that some of these behaviors are more subtle than others. The actions of the child who strives in a subtle manner for any of the goals of misbehavior are characterized by behavior that tends to be disguised, indirect and circuitous. The behavior has a hinting quality about it. In contrast to the above, the child who strives more openly to achieve his goals is rather direct and straight-forward. The child who keeps pulling on Mother's skirt until she notices him is openly demanding attention while the cute, helpless child who just can't seem to do anything by himself is subtly manipulating for the attention of others.

The more discouraged the child (the less worthwhile he feels and the less sure he is of belonging with significant others) the less cooperative he will be and the more he will use goals C and D rather than A and B.

Figure 1

THE ABCD GOALS OF THE MISBEHAVING CHILD

Types of Behavior		The Goals		
More Subtle	More Open	*Immediate Goals	Longer Range Goals	Kind of Belonging
Charming Lazy	Nuisance	A. Attention and service	Belong	Be accepted, respected, worthwhile
Stubborn	Rebellious	B. *Boss*, control have power	Belong	Be accepted, respected, worthwhile
Subtly Vicious	Openly Vicious	C. *Counterhurt*, get revenge, power with vengence	Belong	Notoriety Infamy
Hopeless	Avoidance	D. *Disabled* (get Mother to think this) be left alone.	Belong	No Risk

Feels less sure of his place, less worthwhile, more discouraged. Is less cooperative. →

*The goals by which Mother is manipulated.

Figure 2, Goals of the Behaving-Adjusted Child, is included for comparison purposes.

The persisitent longer-range goal of the misbehaving child is the same as for the behaving child. He wants to belong securely within the family. The immediate goals are those with which Mother should be concerned, for if she helps the misbehaving child achieve them his disturbing behavior will tend to persist.

Goal A-Attention

The child striving for Goal A likes to keep Mother busy with him. Mother's feelings with the child who is misbehaving for attention and service are annoyance and irritation, shown in Figure 3. As Mother interacts with him at this level she finds herself giving undue service, time and attention. She finds herself reminding and coaxing.

The child may operate quite openly in striving for Mother's attention by being the "good child." His good behavior is often at the expense of the other children in the family. He is competitive and usually has poor social relations with others. He may be a perfectionist and have a superior attitude. He feels that Mother will be interested in him and accept him only as long as he has a place better than the others. He often becomes bad when the "bad" child in the family becomes better, for his "goodness" is based on the "badness" of the other. He tends to try to make the other children look bad and clings to a special, favored relationship that he has cultivated with Mother. This child tends to become an adult who is self-righteous, closed, superior and aloof acting, at war with himself and others, and piously belittling of others.

Figure 2

GOALS OF THE BEHAVING-ADJUSTED CHILD

Types of Behavior	Goals		
	Immediate	Longer Range	Kind of Belonging
Constructive			
Cooperative			
Acts benefit child and family members		Belong	Be accepted, respected, worthwhile
Functions horizontally in relation to other family members. (Feels there is room for all. His place and worth are *not* dependent on his pushing others aside or down.)	To be involved cooperatively - constructively with the family.		

Figure 3

GUIDES FOR DISCOVERING THE MISBEHAVING CHILD'S IMMEDIATE GOALS

Goals	Mother's Feelings	Mother's Behavior
(A.) *Attention*, service	Annoyance, irritation	Gives service, attention (reminds, coaxes, etc.) ("You take so much of my time.")
B. *Boss*, have control, have power	Anger	Fights for control, or to be Boss ("You can't get away with that.")
C. *Counterhurt*, get revenge	Hurt	Hurts back, strikes back ("I'll get even.")
D. *Disabled*, to be thought of as such, to be left alone	Despair, feelings of hopelessness	Hesitates to require anything of the child. Leaves child alone. ("I don't know what to do.")

Evidence

The child operating in an open fashion as he strives for goal A may make himself a nuisance by doing obnoxious and irritating things, which causes Mother to keep busy with him constantly. Such behaviors as making messes while Mother is on the phone, losing articles of clothing, and being unable to dress himself serve this purpose nicely.

The child operating more subtly as he strives for Goal A may work at charming others and/or being submissive, dependent, and lazy. Girls tend to use these more subtle methods more than boys. The danger of Mother getting involved with the child in dependent ways is that the child loses his self-respect. He defers to others, which leads to others running his life. He soon feels worthless and unhappy.

Goal B — to Boss Mother, Have Power Over Her

The child who is striving for Goal B, to be boss, have control and power, is more discouraged than the one striving for Goal A. The child generally tries to show Mother who is boss when his involvement techniques, as he tries to get attention and service, fail. If he can't get attention or service from Mother, he makes himself a potent force within the family by controlling others to his own advantage. The child may imitate a powerful Mother or Father and equate being of worth with being powerful.

Mother cannot win a power contest with her child, for if she defeats him she has taught him that power is important. Also, the fact that Mother enters into a struggle for power tells the child that power is important. If she loses in the power struggle her child defeats her and this becomes a payoff that reinforces him to value power.

The child who is rewarded for bossing others learns that his worthwhileness is only as great as his power to control others. In reality he repels them, for people do not like to be controlled. As he alienates others, he struggles even harder, for he illogically reasons that more power will bring people closer to him. A vicious circle is set up. The very things he wants most — respect, love, and a place with others — he prevents from happening.

The child who strives to be boss can do it openly or subtly. The rebellious child who openly disobeys tends to be more direct and straight forward. The stubborn, passive child is more subtle.

As shown in Figure 3, Mother usually feels anger as a response to the child whose goal is to be boss. Her overt behavior tends to be a fight for control. Mother says to the child openly or under her breath, "You can't get away with that."

Goal C — to Counterhurt, Get Revenge

The child striving to counterhurt, get revenge, is more discouraged than the one who is striving for Goal A or B. This child believes that life is unfair. He has feelings of being hurt by others. He has probably been defeated in his struggle for power and retaliates to get even. He may feel ostracized and disliked by others in the family. The child who establishes a revengeful pattern of behavior believes he can belong only by achieving a position of notoriety and infamy. To be hated becomes his novel, unique, accepted place. It is as if he were to say to himself that it is better to be hated than to be ignored or defeated. Viciousness is the only path he sees open to him and he therefore feels triumphant when he can hurt Mother.

If Mother shows hurt or strikes back at the child, she is actually paying him off by saying in effect, "Yes, your perception is true. People are unfair, people hurt, and you can hurt Mother." She may even communicate, "I'll get even."

A child counter-hurting can be openly or subtly vicious as he attempts to hurt Mother. The openly vicious child is more easily identified. The child who says, "I hate you Mother" or who rips up Mother's best dress is being openly vicious. The more subtle ways the child has of hurting Mother may not be so easy to detect. The child who says, "How come you favor Jane over me" is subtly communicating, "You're not a good mother."

Goal D — to appear Disabled (to get Mother to think this)

The goal of the child is to get Mother to think he is disabled so she will give up on him and leave him alone. He is a child who has been successfully beaten down as he tried all the other goals. He has experienced failure in his attempts to find his own worth and a place in the family. He has stopped trying. He hides behind feelings of inferiority and telegraphs to other people that he is unable and can't. He may openly and actively avoid any kind of responsibility to prevent the possibilities of his experiencing further humiliation. Or he may more subtly communicate such hopelessness that others avoid giving him any kind of responsibility.

It is very rare to find a child who has completely given up. Usually, a child operates at this level in certain situations only. His discouragement is usually not complete. Mother usually feels despair and hopelessness when the child acts in this way. She may hesitate to require anything of him and will leave him alone. She says to herself and to the child, "I don't know what to do."

Most children will strive for each of these various goals in certain kinds of situations and Mother need not be too concerned if they are generally responding cooperatively in the family. However, if a child begins to establish a pattern of striving for any one of the ABCD goals, it is imperative that Mother change her behavior to stimulate change in the child's misbehavior. The purpose of this chapter is to give Mother some specific suggestions:

Which Goal: A, B, C or D?

Figures 3 and 1 give some helps for Mother in determining which of the four goals the misbehaving child is aiming at. If Mother finds that she feels annoyed and irritated and is giving much undue service and attention, the child is probably manipulating this from her through his misbehavior. His goal is Goal A.

Evidence for the child functioning at Goal B, to boss, is discovered by again looking to Mother's feelings and behavior. If she feels angry and finds herself quarreling with him, the chances are good that he is striving to boss Mother and have power over her.

When Mother feels hurt as she interacts with her misbehaving child and finds herself hurting the child or feeling, "I'll get even," she has good evidence that the child is functioning at level C. He wants to counterhurt by hurting her as he feels he has been hurt.

Mother's feelings and actions indicate when the misbehaving child is operating at Goal D. When Mother feels hopeless and has feelings of despair and finds herself hesitating to require anything of him, she has good evidence he is trying to get her to ignore him and not demand anything of him. He wants her to assume he is disabled.

What Should Mother Do?

If the child is misbehaving to force Mother to give him attention, she should ignore it, as shown in Figure 4. This means the child's misbehavior should not be seen or recognized in any way. It is as if Mother were to say, "I refuse to see you or interact with you at this mutually disrespectful level." If the child is demanding that Mother do for him things he can do for himself as a method of keeping her busy with him (undue service), she should refuse. She might say "You can do it yourself, Johnny."

Mother should refuse to be drawn into the power struggle with the child who is trying to find his worth by bossing her. The child striving for Goal B should be ignored. By Mother refusing to play his power game, she creates a vacuum and the child, not having anyone to struggle with, eventually gives up. A phrase such as, "You may be right," indicates to the child that you will not play his game. Leaving the area is a way of showing the child that you respect yourself and him too much to allow yourself to be drawn into a power struggle, which is a disrespectful relationship.

Figure 4

A GENERAL GUIDE FOR RESPONDING TO THE MISBEHAVING CHILD

A.B.C.D. Goals of Misbehaving Child	Mother's First Impulse Response (This Rewards Misbehavior)	Mother; Do the Unexpected (This will diminish/stop the Misbehavior)	To Encourage Good Behavior
A. to get *Attention*, wants service or to keep Mother busy.	Mother gives undue attention and/or service ("You take so much of my time.").	Ignore the child at this time. Say nothing. Do nothing. Control facial expression, tone of voice, and body movements which would indicate the child has "got you going." In undue service say, "You're big enough to do it by yourself."	Have positive experiences with the child when he is not demanding involvement, not trying to defeat or hurt you.
B. to *Boss*, control, have power to defeat.	Mother fights for control to be boss. ("You can't get away with that.")	Refuse to engage in a power contest, e.g., say "You could be right." Continue what you are doing. Walk into another room. Lower your sails.	
C. to *Counterhurt*, get revenge, power with vengeance.	Mother hurts back, strikes back. (I'll get even with you.")	Refuse to engage the child in a battle of retaliation. Show no hurt in words, tone of voice, facial expression, body movements, or in any way. Say calmly such things as, "It may be so." Go for a walk.	Set your expectations such that he can have many success experiences. Help him to see that effort is valuable in and of itself.
D. to appear *Disabled* (get Mother to think this, be left alone).	Mother leaves the child alone. Hesitates to require anything of him. ("I don't know what to do.")	Refuse to give up. Keep encouraging the child to try.	

Mother should not show hurt in any way when the misbehaving child counterhurts. If she does, she meets his expectations and reinforces the very misbehavior she wishes to discourage. Mother should also not ridicule or punish in an attempt to get even with the child for such behavior is exactly what the child may be trying to manipulate from Mother to prove she is unfair and his view, that she hurts him, is right.

The most difficult child for Mother to correct is the one who has set a pattern of striving for Goal D. This child is so discouraged he wants to give up trying. He tries to get Mother to give up on him so that nothing is required of him. Mother should refuse to see the child disabled and continue to have faith and trust in his ability to grow and progress even though he no longer has faith in himself. Persistence and the setting of standards for the child which he feels he can reach are important in helping this child. Mother should be encouraged with small progress at first. It will tend to start slow, then pick up as she keeps working with him and exhibits her faith in his ability.

Have Positive Experiences

In essence, the previous suggestions call for a refusal to be manipulated by the misbehaving child. The general guideline for all except those striving for goal D has been to ignore him and refuse to interact when he is attempting to manipulate. Mother should remember, however, that the misbehaving child is not sure of belonging in the family and that his misbehaviors are misguided attempts to belong. Misbehaviors are like red flags signaling the discouragement of the child. Therefore, though Mother refuses to be manipulated, she should realize his discouragement and plan for positive interaction with him at times other than when he is demanding involvement by misbehaving. *The objective is to stimulate increased feelings of belonging and thus make misbehavior unnecessary.*

Some Specific Misbehaviors of the Child

Several specific misbehaviors of children are analyzed in this section. A typical disturbing behavior is presented and Mother is asked to guess the goal of the child and select from two alternatives the response that would tend to correct the misbehavior. Answers are then given and a general discussion concludes each unit. This procedure gives Mother the opportunity to practice identifying the child's goals and responding to correct the child's misbehavior. In cases where the child seems to be striving for two goals at one time, e.g. to boss mother and to counterhurt her, goals B and C, the goal which indicates the most discouragement is to be selected as the right answer. In the above situation, the right answer is goal C. Practice in encouraging good behavior is included in the next section, *Some Additional Practice Cases*.

Rather than reading the whole chapter, Mother may wish to read first about those misbehaviors that have relevance for her disturbing child.

Always Under Foot

Nine-year-old Sarah is the youngest in a family of five. She always seems to be under foot. She smiles sweetly and agrees with everything anyone says. People refer to her as being "cute," a real "charmer." However, she cannot seem to do anything well on her own. Mother asked her to sweep the floor. As usual she failed to do a decent job and mother had to sweep it over. Mother feels irritated and annoyed.

The goal of the child is:

> ....✓.... A. to get Attention, keep Mommy busy with her, get service.

> .... B. to Boss Mommy, have power, defeat her.

> .... C. to Counterhurt, get revenge, power with vengence.

> .... D. to appear Disabled (get Mommy to think this).

To change the child's misbehavior Mother should:

> .... 1. Tell her that any job worth doing is worth doing well.

> ....✓.... 2. Not sweep the floor herself. She should do nothing and say nothing.

Answers: A, 2.

The child who is always underfoot is striving for Goal A, Attention. It is a technique often used by the smaller or younger child. If he makes leaning on others a habit, he will develop feelings of incompetence and worthlessness, for he will not have learned to cope with life by himself.

It is suggested that Mother refuse to give service demanded by the child. She is not to do for the child what he can do for himself. She should encourage the child to take pride in being independent. Phrases such as, "I'm sure you can do it," "Try it; all you need is practice," will do much to help this child.

Getting Mom and Dad to Argue

A typical scene in the Jones' house: Dad told eight-year-old Jean to quit stalling and dry the dishes. She ran crying in to Mother and buried her face in Mother's lap. Mother told Father not to be so hard to Jean. Dad started to yell, "No one does any work around here." Jean cried harder.

The child's goal is:

.... A. to get Attention, keep Mommy busy with her, get service.

.... B. to Boss Mommy, have power, defeat her.

.... C. to Counterhurt, get revenge, power with vengence.

.... D. to appear Disabled (get Mommy to think this).

To change the child's misbehavior Mother should:

.... 1. Ignore Jean. Say no more than, "It's between you and your father Jean," and continue to straighten up the living room.

.... 2. Tell Father not to expect so much of Jean.

Answers: B, 1.

Arguments between Mother and Father are often stimulated by the child's goals for power. Mother has a tendency to indulge the child while Father sometimes has a tendency to be overly strict. The reverse may occur. Whatever the case, there is a tendency of the more permissive parent to compensate for the overstrictness of the other. The child soon learns to manipulate the overpermissive parent and cause him or her to come to his aid. He will often stimulate the strict parent to strictness in order to get comfort and service from the protecting other parent. Mother and Father should not interfere with one another's discipline.

The author is reminded of Jill, a ten-year old girl with two younger brothers. Her father was very demanding and Mother, feeling she should protect Jill from her father, was over-protective. Jill would run sobbing to Mother after being disciplined by Father. Jill was able to get special attention and concern from Mother and to defeat Father through manipulating pity and sympathy from Mother who allowed her to avoid complying with Father's requests. Jill found her own worth through being powerful.

The procedure used in dealing with such a child is to restrict Mother's and Father's conflicts to them only and refuse to allow any of the children to move in. If the child does "trigger" or get involved in the arguments and disputes, Mother and Father should unite and expel the child. It is generally better for parents to agree on methods of child discipline. However, if they cannot agree, they should not interfere with one another's disciplining. Mother should respect Father's disciplining even though she may not agree. Father should also respect Mother in her disciplining even though he does not agree. One parent should not compensate for the strictness of the other or interfere with the other's disciplining, for the child quickly learns to stir up conflict to his own advantage.

Bedwetting

Bob is seven. He has two younger brothers ages three and one. He has wet his bed almost every night for two years. Mother scolds and punishes, but he continues. As usual Mother got up during the night at twelve and three to take him to the bathroom. At twelve the bed was wet. When she took him to the bathroom at three, he turned and wet all over her leg and floor. Mother started to cry and said, "How could you do that?"

The child's goal is:

....   A. to get Attention, keep Mommy busy with him, get service.

....   B. to Boss Mommy, have power, defeat her.

....   C. to Counterhurt, get revenge, power with vengence.

....   D. to appear Disabled (get Mommy to think this).

To change the child's misbehavior Mother should:

....   1. Take Bob to the bathroom more often. Concentrate on giving him fewer liquids.

....   2. Say nothing to him about his bedwetting. Mother, get a good night's sleep. Have Bob put his wet sheets and clothes in the washer.

Answers: C, 2.

The child who wets his bed pursues Goal C, to counter-hurt. Usually bedwetting is not due to organic problems of the child; however, a good medical examination is necessary to insure that no organic deficiency is involved. Bedwetting is more often due to problems in interpersonal relationships between the child and his parents. The child bedwetter is antagonistic and revengeful. He is one who hides behind a mask of self-abasement as he seeks revenge. His ambition is to make as big a mess and be as dirty as possible. He doesn't wash. He usually is a very discouraged child, disgusted with himself and those about him. He keeps everyone concerned and frustrated with him for no one knows what to do. The dismay of others and their frustration and hurt is his payoff, his satisfaction. It is usually directed at Mother. Mother is the one who cleans up the bed, washes off the child, grumbles over him, is embarrassed by him, and is made to feel inadequate.

Bob's goal, in the case described above, is to hurt Mother as he feels she has hurt him by giving more attention to his two younger brothers than to him. He may illogically think Mother no longer loves him as much as she does them. He feels hurt and seeks to hurt Mother by causing her difficulties through his bedwetting.

A problem of the bedwetter is that he "cons" almost everyone, including the professionals. No one seems to know what to do.

Mother should not take special pains with the bedwetter. She should calmly ignore him. She should not set the alarm in the middle of the night to get up and help him. She should not show hurt nor embarrassment, because this is what the child wants. As well as not punishing, Mother should not praise him when he does not wet the bed. Praise emphasizes her concern, which the child can then manipulate to his own advantage. Praise tells him, "My wetting the bed is important to Mother." So when he wants to hurt, he knows what to do.

If the child is old enough, Mother should not clean the bed for him. He should clean up the mess himself. He should be treated no differently than the other children. Mother's over-concern and over-solicitude creates a special place for the bedwetter and encourages bedwetting further.

Criticism or repudiation of the child discourages him. Mother should realize that the bedwetter is very discouraged and, therefore, work at increasing his self-reliance and independence. *She should help the child feel that he belongs securely within the family so that he will not want to counterhurt.* Getting involved with him in pleasant ways will tend to encourage him. Mother's sense of humor encourages a sense of humor in the child and is helpful. *He must be encouraged to have faith in himself and in other people.*

In summary, Mother should be as little involved with the child over his bedwetting as possible. He should take the responsibility of cleaning himself and the bed. Mother should work hard at stimulating the child to a greater self-respect by having him do more things on his own and getting involved with him in positive ways.

Biting Fingernails

Jackie, a ten-year-old, is the oldest in a family of six. Her fingernails are bitten down to the quick. Today, as usual, Mother saw her biting her fingernails and said, "Stop that Jackie. How can you continue to bite your fingernails when it makes your hands look so awful? I never did that when I was your age." Jackie immediately took her hand away from her mouth, but as soon as Mother looked away she continued biting them.

The child's goal is:

.... A. to get Attention, keep Mommy busy with her, get service.

.... B. to Boss Mommy, have power, defeat her.

.... C. to Counterhurt, get revenge, power with vengence.

.... D. to appear Disabled (get Mommy to think this).

To change the child's misbehavior Mother should:

.... 1. Not see the misbehavior, continue ironing.

.... 2. Tell her that boys will not like her when she gets older if she continues.

Answers: A, 1.

The goal of the child who bites his fingernails is usually A, to get attention. Mother can discover the purposes of the child who bites his nails by looking to her own behavior. Nail biting usually embarrasses her and she finds herself continually telling him to stop it. This keeps her busy and involved with him. When this kind of interaction is carried to the extreme, it ends in a power conflict to see who is going to be boss. The child then hides behind a mask of nervousness as he defeats Mother. Nail biting is a way of engaging Mother.

The procedure that Mother can follow to correct this kind of behavior is to do nothing and say nothing about the nail biting itself. She is to realize, however, that nail biting is a red flag. The child is actually saying he is not sure of his place and that this is his way of getting Mother to pay attention to him. *Mother should try to see how the child perceives things and take time with him in enjoyable activities. An occasional arm around the shoulder, a hug, and squeeze when he is not manipulating for attention by biting his nails will help the child feel that he belongs.*

Brutality

Sammy, a seven-year-old, is the third of six children. He has an older brother and sister. Five years separate him from a younger sister, and three from a younger brother. Sammy always seems to beat up on the younger children, mar the furniture, and destroy everything he touches. Today was a typical day. Sammy was playing with his four-year old brother and, as Mother was looking out the window, he took a board and hit his little brother over the head. Mother ran out crying and said, "How could you be so mean?" Later today, Mother caught Sammy cutting a hole in her favorite table cloth. She broke down sobbing.

The child's goal is:

.... A. to get Attention, keep Mommy busy with him, get service.

.... B. to Boss Mommy, have power, defeat her.

.... C. to Counterhurt, get revenge, power with vengence.

.... D. to appear Disabled (get Mommy to think this).

To change the child's misbehavior Mother should:

.... 1. Quietly but firmly separate the two and not allow them to play together until they both agree to play cooperatively.

.... 2. Spank Sammy and put him to bed. Do not allow him to play with his younger brother until he agrees to be nice.

Answers: C, 1.

The goal of the child who is brutal and vicious is Goal C. He wants to counterhurt because he feels he has been hurt. Sammy felt he had no place in the family. He did not have the privileges of the older nor the service from Mother which the younger received. Through being brutal and violent he forced Mother to get involved with him and was also able to hurt her as he felt she had hurt him.

The brutal child may resist order by using his anger to disrupt and wreck the family. He also sees life as unfair and feels he is treated unfairly. He feels hurt and strikes out to get revenge.

It is found that parents of a brutal child are often brutal themselves and/or excessively strict. Over-indulging parents also tend to raise brutal children. The indulging mother pampers and spoils the child by giving in to his every whim and demand. Mother's pampering and indulgence increases the dependency of the child, which increases his anger and resentment. The results are feelings of worthlessness and dependency. He fights back which he feels is his right. He may become a tyrannical monster.

Neglect can also result in a brutal child. The mother who is too busy with community affairs, clubs and church work communicates to him that she thinks other things are more important. This hurts him deeply and he strives to hurt back.

Mother should not allow the brutal, vicious child to hurt or intimidate her. She should ignore his behavior if at all possible and not let him know that he can hurt her. If the child is very destructive, the environment can be arranged in such a way that the damage he does is inconsequential. If he becomes too destructive, Mother can give him a choice of either settling down or going to the time-out room. She should tell him that as soon as he decides to behave he can come out. If the child does not cooperate, Mother is to remove him firmly, but gently, to the room.

Mother should take some positive steps. One is to see through the eyes of the child by perceiving his world, including his relationship with her. *Through kindness, gentleness and affection when the child is quiet, Mother can talk with him and thereby improve the relationship.* This is very important because the child is saying in his brutality and violence that he feels life is unfair and that people he loves are unfair to him. He is hurting so he wants to hurt back.

If the child is large and the brutality and destructiveness is too great, the parents may have to remove the child from the family and send him to a special home. This, however, would be only under extreme circumstances.

There are many things in our society which foster brutality. One is the masculinity concept found among some of our subgroups who teach that to be a man one must be aggressive and somewhat brutal. TV and the movies encourage brutality as they glamorize crime and violence. They teach the child that through violence and brutality, excitement can be had. Our society also tends to teach that power, which begets violence, is of great value. Violence and brutality are very often an imitation of parental behavior. Brutality begets brutality.

Correcting Mother

Rhea, who is eleven ,is the oldest. Mother was discussing with a neighbor about a talk that was given in sacrament meeting the previous evening. She said, "It was a good talk. I enjoyed it thoroughly. It really gave my spirits a lift."

Rhea spoke up, "Mother it wasn't a good talk. He didn't know what he was talking about, and besides, he kept looking at his notes."

Mother responded, "Well I thought it was a good talk. I don't think you know what you're talking about. Go in the house."

The child's goal is:

.... A. to get Attention, keep Mommy busy with her, get service.

.... B. to Boss Mommy, have power, defeat her.

.... C. to Counterhurt, get revenge, power with vengence.

.... D. to appear Disabled (get Mommy to think this).

To change the child's misbehavior Mother should:

.... 1. Say calmly, "You may be right."

.... 2. Tell her she was wrong and send her in the house.

Answers: B, 1.

The child who sets a pattern of correcting Mother is striving for Goal B. He wants to show who is boss.

The author is reminded of another eleven-year old child whom we will call Jill. On one occasion she was riding with her Mother and Father to enjoy the beautiful mountain scenery. Mother started to describe the color and name of a bush that was growing along the mountainside. Jill retorted, as she usually did, "Mother, you're wrong, you don't know what you're talking about." Mother told her to shut up and not be so stupid. A verbal battle began.

Undoubtedly, Jill is discouraged. She is not sure of her place in the family. She feels that in order to be worthwhile she has to be boss. Mother became engaged with her on her level and this further intensified Jill's feelings of not belonging and inadequacy.

As in all power struggles, Mother should refuse to become engaged. A response which shows your refusal may be, "You may be right." Avoid the battle. Do not engage in the disrespectful power-oriented relationship. Realize that the child who continues to correct you is unsure of himself and is discouraged. He is mistakenly trying to improve his worth by defeating you.

Mother should foster an active program for helping the child to become more sure of himself. One way is to interact warmly with him when he is not obnoxious. *Do all you can to increase the child's feelings of self-worth by actively seeking ways in which he can contribute responsibly and cooperatively to the welfare of the family.*

Dependence

Six-year-old John never completely dresses himself in the morning. Today he came down from his bedroom, as usual, with his shoe laces untied. Mother tied them for him. She has demonstrated over and over to him how to do it, but he does not learn.

The child's goal is:

.... A. to get Attention, keep Mommy busy with him, get service.

.... B. to Boss Mommy, have power, defeat her.

.... C. to Counterhurt, get revenge, power with vengence.

.... D. to appear Disabled (get Mommy to think this).

To change the child's misbehavior Mother should:

.... 1. Take more time to train him how to tie his shoe laces.

.... 2. Do not see they are untied.

Answers: A, 2.

The dependent child is striving for Goal A. He begs for special attention and service. He gets others to remind him and do much for him. Another characteristic of this child is that he tends to do things poorly in the hope that they will be redone by Mother. He is slow and may appear to take a long time to learn anything.

Mothers of such children are often demanding and perfectionistic. They tend to take over all the domestic responsibilities in the family and do all for their children. This makes them an easy mark for the dependent child.

If Mother is to increase the independence of the child, she must not allow him to get her to do things for him that he can do for himself. *She should take time to give him responsibility in the family so that he feels he is of worth and of value.* She should ignore his inabilities and sloppiness. She should also realize that adult standards may be too discouraging for the child. She should allow and expect the child to make some mistakes as he learns to do things for himself.

Destroy Property

John took a knife and made a deep cut in the walnut wood of the sofa arm. Mother yelled, spanked him soundly and then sent him to his room.

The child's goal is:

.... A. to get Attention, keep Mommy busy with him, get service.

.... B. to Boss Mommy, have power, defeat her.

.... C. to Counterhurt, get revenge, power with vengence.

.... D. to appear Disabled (get Mommy to think this).

To change the child's misbehavior Mother should:

.... 1. Have Father spank him when he gets home.

.... 2. Quietly work out a way with John that so much of his allowance goes toward refinishing the arm.

Answers: C, 2.

The goal of the child who purposely breaks and mars property is that of Goal C, to Counterhurt. He strikes out and hurts back since he feels he has been hurt. Often he is revengeful in very powerful ways and ends up tyrannizing the family. Often parents are cowed and completely "buffaloed" by him.

Procedures which can be used with this child in correcting his misbehavior are similar to those used with the vicious and brutal. Mother should arrange the environment in such a manner that he cannot get to her through his destructiveness. She should ignore his misbehavior as much as possible. However, if he becomes too destructive, he should be given the choice of respecting the property of others or going to the time-out room. He can come out when he decides that he will be respectful. This is done in a gentle, but firm manner. Mother may want to use the phrase, "I know it's hard for you but you must learn you can't destroy other people's property." If he is old enough, he should make restitution for that which he has destroyed.

An example of a positive approach would be this: Mother could talk to him quietly at other times such as bedtime to see how he feels and thinks. *She should get involved with him at times when he is behaving cooperatively.* This will take special effort on Mother's part because the child who is destructive fatigues her and creates emotions that make it difficult for her to respond to him in positive ways. However, this child needs it more than the others, for he feels that people have hurt him and that life is unfair. In addition, he is not sure that constructive behavior will win for him a secure position in the family.

The Disobedient Child

Mother told John, age seven, to hurry and get dressed for Sunday School. John said, "I won't, I am not going, and no one can make me."

The child's goal is:

....   A. to get Attention, keep Mommy busy with him, get service.

....   B. to Boss Mommy, have power, defeat her.

....   C. to Counterhurt, get revenge, power with vengence.

....   D. to appear Disabled (get Mommy to think this).

To change the child's misbehavior Mother should:

....   1. Say, "Listen young man, you are going if I have to drag you."

....   2. Say nothing. Two minutes before time to leave, announce the time to the family. Leave without John if he is not ready.

Answers: B, 2.

John wants to show Mother who is boss in an open, confrontive manner. If she responds with, "Listen young man, you are going if I have to drag you," she is feeding into a power struggle which will reinforce the child's misbehavior. By ignoring his words of battle, Mother refuses to become engaged. By her leaving on time, whether John is ready or not, he learns to experience the consequences of his own behavior. John's desire to be with the family and friends will be enough motivation for him to get ready if he *knows* Mother will leave with or without him.

The child who sets a pattern of disobeying Mother is typically operating at Goal B, striving to be boss. The typical and most frequent expression of the child's revolt against cooperation and order in the family is that of disobedience. Mother should realize, however, that healthy children, because of their creativity and God-given free agency, will occasionally disobey. The child who continually obeys unquestioningly is cowed and dispirited. Mother's behaviors that stimulate the child to disobedience are impatience, indulgence, spoiling, indecisiveness and inconsistency. Violence, humiliation, many demands and repetition of orders also stimulate him to develop patterns of disobedience.

Children will often support one another in their disobedience, especially if their ages are close and they are of the same sex. This gives them added power, an added sense of importance. The author is reminded of one family where three boys, ages eight, ten, and eleven, were able to defeat their Mother at almost every turn as they supported one another in their drives to boss her.

Mother should first clear away the hostile atmosphere as she attempts to deal effectively with a child like John. If he refuses to mind, she should not order unnecessarily.

The disobedient child is also saying that he is unsure of his own place; therefore, *Mother should go to him when he is not disobeying and talk with him to show her love and interest for him.* The use of natural and logical consequences can be very helpful in working with the child who is disobedient. An example is the child who is always late for supper. Mother should only call him once. If he does not arrive in time, the food is put away after everyone has finished and the child goes without. No service of a special individual supper is given this child as it would pay off his disobedience.

Fear and Anxiety

Six-year-old Joan is an only child. Whenever Mother and Father want to go out for an evening together, leaving Joan home with a baby sitter, she screams, cries, and says, "You don't love me. You'll never come back." She seems so fearful that Mother and Father usually decide not to leave.

The child's goal is:

.... A. to get Attention, keep Mommy busy with her, get service.

.... B. to Boss Mommy, have power, defeat her.

.... C. to Counterhurt, get revenge, power with vengence.

.... D. to appear Disabled (get Mommy to think this).

To change the child's misbehavior Mother should:

.... 1. Calm her down by staying home and fixing her hot chocolate and toast.

.... 2. Say "I know its hard, but you'll learn," then leave as planned.

Answers: B, 2.

The goal of the child using anxiety and fear is B, to boss Mother. Fear seems to be at the root of all neurotic phenomena. Some fear is quite common to all children; however, it can become a severe problem depending upon how Mother responds to the child when he is fearful. Fear is a communication of helplessness and is often used by the only child. It is often used by the child who feels threatened by a newborn baby. It is also used by the child experiencing difficulty in competing with older or more efficient brothers and sisters.

When Mother responds to the child's fear with sympathy or pity, she reinforces the fearful behavior and it tends to become more firmly entrenched. The more Mother expresses concern, the greater the payoff.

Through his fears the child learns to tyrannize Mother — at times the whole family, as in the case of Joan. The child gets Mother to respond to his every wish and demand. Dependency, service, and tyranny are the results of anxiety and fear that are reinforced.

What procedures can Mother use when the child is fearful? First of all, she should play it down and not react emotionally to it. She should be calm and casual. If the fear is of the dark, a night light is helpful.

When Mother reacts emotionally she rewards the child. Her emotional concern expresses to him, "You should be concerned." Mother's anxiety concerning his fear is much more dangerous than the child's fear for her anxiety will stimulate him to greater levels of fear. Mother is to give him love and attention when he is *not* fearful and respond calmly when he is afraid.

Usually the fearful child is spoiled and pampered and unsure of himself. *Mother should be less indulgent and stimulate him to more self-reliance and independence.*

The "Good" Child

Eleven-year-old Sue, the oldest of four children, came running to Mother and said, "Jane and Sheryl are fighting again. You better come quick or they will be getting their dresses all dirty."

The child's goal is:

.... A. to get Attention, keep Mommy busy with her, get service.

.... B. to Boss Mommy, have power, defeat her.

.... C. to Counterhurt, get revenge, power with vengence.

.... D. to appear Disabled (get Mommy to think this).

To change the child's misbehavior Mother should:

.... 1. Say nothing. Continue cutting out cookies.

.... 2. Praise Sue for being such a good child. Stop Jane and Sheryl from fighting.

Answers: A, 1.

Many mothers are most easily "conned" by the "good child." This child usually allies with her under the guise of helping when she is having difficulty with the other children. The purpose of the child's good behavior is to get attention and special involvement from Mother at the expense of the others. The goodness of the child is for the purpose of being superior as he displaces the other children for a favored position with Mother. He tends to be perfect and always correct. He tends to have poor social relationships with others. He must win or he will not play. He criticizes others and points up other's faults to Mother. This child's goodness is not for goodness itself, constructive and cooperative behavior. It is for praise from Mother in being better than the others. In counseling with families who are having difficulty, we find that when Mother establishes a better relationship with the "bad" child, the "good" child often becomes bad for he sees himself belonging safely only as the others are in trouble with Mother. He operates on the vertical, not the horizontal plane. This child is discouraged.

Procedures which can be used by Mother with the "good" child include not allowing him to ally with her when she is having difficulty with one of the other children. She should treat all of them as a group when there are difficulties. There should be no third parties in the family mediating between Mother and other misbehaving children. Mother should not listen to his criticism of the other children's "bad" behavior. She is to say nothing.

A positive thing Mother can do is to chat with him, when he is not cutting others down, about those things that are of interest to him. This child should be supported and encouraged when he is behaving responsibly and cooperatively in the family.

Ineptitude

Tim, age six, is the second child. He is small for his age. Each morning as school time approaches he complains of having a stomach-ache. "Whenever I ask him to read for me," Mother said, "he gets a panicky look in his eyes and sort of melts into the chair. It's got so I don't like to ask him to do anything."

The child's goal is:

.... A. to get Attention, keep Mommy busy with him, get service.

.... B. to Boss Mommy, have power, defeat her.

.... C. to Counterhurt, get revenge, power with vengence.

.... D. to appear Disabled (get Mommy to think this).

To change the child's misbehavior Mother should:

.... 1. Tell him to shape up and that his older brother Joe does not act that way.

.... 2. Ignore his stomach ache. Say, "I know it's hard to learn to read, but you'll learn with practice." Never criticize.

Answers: D, 2.

The child who exhibits general ineptitude is operating at Goal D. He wants to be considered disabled and left alone. The young child is faced with many difficulties in the world. He has many new things to learn. He also finds the people he loves to be demanding and critical. If Mother is demanding, critical, practices improper training techniques and does not allow the child to experience much success, he will perceive himself as unable and give up. When he exhibits ineptitude, Mother reinforces his belief if she feels and believes this too. His feeling of inadequacy then increases. The picture becomes complicated when Mother feels guilty about the problems or handicaps the child has as a result of accidents or early sickness. A guilty Mother will often do things for the child that increase his feelings of ineptitude.

This child is difficult to work with. Mother must be patient and understanding. She must encourage him to be self-reliant in the small things first and then in the larger things as he experiences some success. She should pace her expectations to his feelings that he has a good chance of achieving them.

Mother should provide opportunities for the child to develop his talents. As he practices, Mother should never criticize him. Often the child will get interested in those areas in which the other children have no interest. These are areas where he feels there is less danger of competition. As he meets success in building his talents it will tend to generalize to other areas as he develops a feeling of competence and worthwhileness.

There are very few children who are really unable or who have no abilities. For example, it is found that many in America believe themselves to be tone deaf. As far as the author is concerned, this generally is in error. People are discouraged but very few are truly tone deaf. The author is reminded of the fact that learning the Chinese language requires the ability to hear four distinct tones. Many Americans "can't" learn it because they are "tone deaf." However, it is interesting to note that there are few if any Chinese who cannot learn the language because of tone deafness. Each child can develop a number of different abilities. Each child has a tremendous potential which is unfortunately little tapped in our society.

Mother should not allow herself to be manipulated by the child to a position of discouragement and hopelessness where she no longer has any expectations for him. It takes patience and sensitivity to get the child to believe in himself. She should realize that small advances at first may be relatively great strides forward and she should not be discouraged by them. *If mother persists, is kind and gentle but firm, her child will eventually make good progress.*

Leaving Toys Around

Five-year-old Jimmy leaves his toys scattered all over the house. When Mother tells him to pick them up, he starts putting them away. But as soon as she leaves, he quits. Mother finds herself constantly nagging.

The child's goal is:

....   A. to get Attention, keep Mommy busy with him, get service.

....   B. to Boss Mommy, have power, defeat her.

....   C. to Counterhurt, get revenge, power with vengence.

....   D. to appear Disabled (get Mommy to think this).

To change the child's misbehavior Mother should:

....   1. Tell Jimmy dad will spank him when he gets home if he does not pick up his toys immediately.

....   2. When toys are found scattered around, pick them up yourself and store them away. Give them to Jimmy when he agrees to put them in his toy box when he is finished playing with them.

Answers: A, 2.

The child who continues to leave his toys scattered
around where Mother can trip over them is probably striving for Goal A. He just never gets around to putting his
toys back where they belong and Mother finds herself nagging and keeping after him to do it. This is the purpose of
his misbehavior, to keep Mother busy with him.

Mother should ask the child only once to put his toys
away. Her voice is calm, but firm. If he refuses, Mother
locks them away in a place where the child cannot get them.
He is told that he can have them as soon as he agrees to
put them back in the toy box when he is finished playing.
Mother does this not to retaliate, but for training the child
and the preservation of order. As the child learns to take
responsibility for a few toys, he is given more, but only to
the extent he demonstrates responsible behavior. If the
child leaves his toys out after they have been put away by
Mother and then returned to him, she should keep them
stored away for a longer period the second time. The process
is repeated again and again until the child is trained to put
away his toys by himself.

Losing Items

Three-year-old Jamie keeps the whole neighborhood in turmoil. He goes out to play, takes his shoes off and returns home without them. Mother scolds, but it seems to do no good. She takes him by the hand and retraces his steps hunting for them. If there are any neighbors outside at the time, they too become involved in the hunt.

The child's goal is:

    .... A. to get Attention, keep Mommy busy with him, get service.

    .... B. to Boss Mommy, have power, defeat her.

    .... C. to Counterhurt, get revenge, power with vengence.

    .... D. to appear Disabled (get Mommy to think this).

To change the child's misbehavior Mother should:

    .... 1. Say, "Dinner is ready when you get your shoes." He is not allowed in the house until he returns with his shoes.

    .... 2. Ask the neighbors to help you watch where he leaves them.

Answers: A, 1.

One of the most effective ways the child has of keeping Mother busy is to lose items of clothing. The youngster who makes this a habit is usually misbehaving for Goal A, *Attention and/or service*. Mother's over concern for the monetary value of the "lost" item makes her more vulnerable to the goals of the child.

It is suggested that when the child loses his shoes, he suffer the logical consequences of his behavior . His not being allowed back in the house until he returns with his shoes, or Mother's refusal to allow him to play out of doors until he agrees and demonstrates responsibility in taking care of his shoes, are examples of logical consequences.

Whatever course of action Mother chooses, she should watch her tone of voice and the amount of her talking so as to avoid useless involvement. There should be no hint of retaliation.

The child who continually loses items is discouraged or misguided in thinking that this is a good way of getting others involved with him. Mother should help the child by providing ways he can constructively contribute to the welfare of the family. He can help Mother dry dishes, sweep the floor, dust, and etc. *As he learns to contribute constructively, he will think better of himself and others and will have less need to employ useless techniques.*

Lying

Eight-year-old Janet, a youngest child, did not clean the bathtub. Mother told her to do it. Janet said, "I have." Mother responded, "You're lying; go wash the tub." A verbal argument developed with Janet finally stomping into the bathroom.

The child's goal is:

.... A. to get Attention, keep Mommy busy with her, get service.

.... B. to Boss Mommy, have power, defeat her.

.... C. to Counterhurt, get revenge, power with vengence.

.... D. to appear Disabled (get Mommy to think this).

To change the child's misbehavior Mother should:

.... 1. Tell Janet to quit lying, because the bishop wouldn't approve.

.... 2. Say nothing at the time. When Janet wants to watch TV say, "When all your work is done."

Answers: B, 2.

Lying is a device used by children to show Mother who is boss. The child who develops habits of lying usually has forceful and demanding parents. Their high expectations and demands tend to stimulate lying. Lying becomes the child's defense.

Generally Mother's reaction to the child when he lies is one of frustration and anger. With these emotional outbursts she signals to the child that he has a weapon he can use against her.

Mother should check her behavior to see if she is powerful, demanding, and expecting too much of the child.

A first step in correcting lying is to lessen Mother's dominance and control over the child. Some go to the extreme of watching and correcting the child's every move. This stimulates rebellion and lying. She should trust him more by structuring situations so he can do more on his own without depending on her. Mother is to work at establishing positive relationships with the child at times other than during conflict. Usually this is enough to correct the lying. If he continues, Mother can allow him to experience, first hand, the results of lying by being untruthful to him. She may tell him she is going to take him to a movie. Then, the last minute, say she was just lying and refuse to take him. This is done for the purpose of training only and should be devoid of any retaliation. After the child is disappointed, Mother talks with him about his feelings of disappointment suggesting this is one reason why people should not lie to one another.

The very young child has a good imagination and will often not know truth from fiction. The reaction of significant adults will determine, to a great extent, whether or not he learns to use lying to gain misguided goals.

Masturbation

Seven-year-old Stewart is the oldest boy. He has two younger brothers, ages four and three. "From the time he was four years old he has played with his genitals," reported mother. Today, as mother walked passed his room she saw him setting on the edge of his bed stroking his penis. As usual mother said, "How can you do that? It's a filthy, dirty habit." She then slapped him.

The child's goal is:

.... A. to get Attention, keep Mommy busy with him, get service.

.... B. to Boss Mommy, have power, defeat her.

.... C. to Counterhurt, get revenge, power with vengence.

.... D. to appear Disabled (get Mommy to think this).

To change the child's misbehavior Mother should:

.... 1. Walk on past the door. Next day take Stewart shopping with you.

.... 2. Tell him God would be displeased and that what he is doing is very sinful.

The child who masturbates is usually striving for Goal B. It is his way of showing Mother who is boss. The author remembers the case of an only child, a six-year old boy, who drove Mother "crazy" by continual masturbation. His Mother was a perfectionist and controlled the child's every move. She was so powerful the only way the child felt he could assert himself and defeat Mother was through masturbation. Masturbation made her "sick" and, therefore, more vulnerable to defeat. This was about the only area in the child's life where he had some control.

Where masturbation is a problem, Mother should first look at her own behavior. Some Mothers will sexually stimulate the child by establishing a too close, physical contact which turns to her loving and petting him. This may especially occur where there is only one child who is male and there is no father. Also parental over-concern with the child when he is seen handling his genitals will stimulate him. Usually masturbation is used by the child for the primary purpose of defeating Mother. Sexual pleasure is only a secondary purpose.

If Mother is to discourage masturbation, her first step is to make sure she does not interfere when he is masturbating. It should be completely ignored. The child will naturally explore his body and at an early age treat his genitals like any other part unless Mother draws special attention to it through her over-concern. As the child grows Mother should take time to discourage masturbation by discussing it with him when there is a good relationship.

Quarreling

Jane is ten and Joel is eight. It seems to mother that they are always quarreling and fighting. Mother was baking a cake while Joel and Jane were reading in the living room. Suddenly, Jane screamed and came running into where Mother was cooking. She cried, "Mother, Joel hit me again." Mother said, "Joel, you've got to treat your sister with more respect."

The goals of the children are:

.... A. to get Attention, keep Mommy busy with them, get service.

.... B. to Boss Mommy, have power, defeat her.

.... C. to Counterhurt, get revenge, power with vengence.

.... D. to appear Disabled (get Mommy to think this).

To change the child's misbehavior Mother should:

.... 1. Go in and tell Joel to settle down. Give Jane a piece of cake.

.... 2. Keep on with your cooking. Say, "The two of you can work it out."

Answers: A, 2.

Excessive quarreling among children is usually their attempt to keep Mother busy with them or to show Mother who is boss. Goals of quarreling children are usually A or B.

Quarreling is very threatening to "good mothers." We are taught to be a peaceful people. This is good; however, the way many mothers respond to their fighting children usually stimulates more quarreling rather than discouraging it. When Mother intervenes she tends to protect the younger or sickly child and blame the older or more robust. Usually it is the small or sickly who runs to Mother crying and sobbing about how badly he has been treated. This is a very effective way of getting Mother to show preference for him.

Many problems develop when Mother gets involved in children's quarreling:

1. Mother uses much energy in acting as judge, jury, and executioner of the judgment.

2. She can't be fair because she doesn't know the behind-the-scenes maneuvering. Very often it is found that the small or sickly child will provoke the quarrel to get Mother to protect him.

3. Mother's interference adds a powerful, new dimension to the quarreling, which is competition for Mother's show of allegiance.

4. Mother's interference stimulates crying, whimpering, and dependence, which prevents the child from gaining experience and practice in resolving his problems with others.

The advantages of staying out of children's quarrels are:

1. *They gain practice and experience in resolving conflicts.*

2. *It stimulates self-reliance.*

3. *It frees Mother for more positive relationships with all the children.*

Mother should respond to quarreling children by being calm. She can respect herself by not allowing them to drag her into their quarreling. If the quarreling bothers her, she can give them the choice of stopping the fighting or going outside and settling it there. When the small or sickly comes for protection, Mother is to say, "You can work it out." She should treat quarreling children as a group, using phrases such as "OK, you kids, stop your quarreling or take it outside," rather than, "Joel! Stop hitting your sister."

Quarreling and fighting will occur occasionally even with the best of children. If Mother stays out of their quarrels and fights they will quickly learn to work at resolving their difficulties rather than using quarrels to keep Mother busy.

Questions, Questions, Questions

Janette is five. Mother does not know why, but she is often irritated and annoyed with her. The following is typical of much of their conversation.

Janette: "Mommy, can I have an apple?"
Mother: "No."
Janette: "Why not, Mommy?"
Mother: "Because it's too close to supper."
Janette: "Can't you give me just one?"
Mother: "No."
Janette: "Why not, Mommy?"
Mother: "Because I already told you."
Janette: "Mother, can't I have just one apple?"

The child's goal is:

.... A. to get Attention, keep Mommy busy with her, get service.

.... B. to Boss Mommy, have power, defeat her.

.... C. to Counterhurt, get revenge, power with vengence.

.... D. to appear Disabled (get Mommy to think this).

To change the child's misbehavior Mother should:

.... 1. Ignore her after answering once. Say nothing. Continue to prepare supper.

.... 2. Send her to her room.

Answers: A, 1.

It has been an educational practice among many professionals to indoctrinate their students with the idea they should never refuse to answer a child's question, for this will stunt his creativity. This plays into the hands of the child who uses questions for Goal A, to keep Mother busy with him. Using questions is an especially effective way to manipulate Mother to keep her involved, because she tends to feel guilty if she does not answer. She should listen and observe carefully, and if his goal is to keep Mother busy, she should refuse to play his game by not answering. If he persists, Mother may tell him that he really does not want to know. He only wishes to keep her busy. Few words should be spoken, as any kind of involvement can be a payoff that will encourage his questioning behavior.

The Perfectionist

Janice and Jane are ten-year-old twin sisters. Janice does everything well and likes other people to know about it. This evening she came home from school and said, "Look Mother, I got ninety-nine percent in this math test. Jane only got seventy percent."

The child's goal is:

.... A. to get Attention, keep Mommy busy with her, get service.

.... B. to Boss Mommy, have power, defeat her.

.... C. to Counterhurt, get revenge, power with vengence.

.... D. to appear Disabled (get Mommy to think this).

To change the child's misbehavior Mother should:

.... 1. Walk into the bedroom and finish straightening up.

.... 2. Tell her that she did well, but that no doubt Jane worked hard too.

Answers: A, 1.

Goal A was selected as the right answer for Janice because her primary goal is to appear better than Jane for the purpose of getting preferential praise from Mother.

The child who practices perfection in everything he does is usually a discouraged child. The goals which he is striving for are typically A, B, or C. His purposes may be to get attention, defeat, or hurt others. He may strive to gain approval or to defeat Mother and drive her to distraction. This child does everything well, from being meticulous about cleaning his own body, to his school studies and love of order. He stresses his good intentions and excuses his defeats and failures. He has little faith in himself and fears that others will not accept him. He feels as if his behavior is never good enough.

His perfection is usually at the expense of others. He tends to be very competitive and strives to be superior at the expense of those around him. This includes Mother.

If he is a perfectionist for the goal of keeping people busy with him, it is best to ignore his behavior. If he is trying to show who is boss, Mother should withdraw. If he does this to hurt, she should respond by not showing hurt.

If the child persists in his obnoxious, self-righteous, perfectionistic behavior, others will withdraw from him and his fear of not being accepted becomes a reality. As he tries harder in his inept ways to be accepted others will move farther away from him.

It is suggested then that Mother not get involved with the perfectionistic child in either praising him, engaging in power struggles, or hurtful interactions. *The child needs much encouragement at times other than when he is demanding involvement through his perfectionistic behavior.* It is only through actions and words given as free gifts when he is not demanding them that he will learn he is accepted.

Responsibility of Everyone

Eleven-year-old Jerry is an oldest child who is continually telling the other kids what to do. Sometimes he even tells Mother what to do. Tonight after supper Jerry kept saying to the other children such things as, "Joan, that dish isn't clean enough. Jim, it's time for you to sweep the floor. Come on, do a good job. You're sure sloppy. Here let me show you how to do that. Mother, you didn't wrap the meat up well enough that you put in the fridge."

The child's goal is:

.... **A.** to get Attention, keep Mommy busy with him, get service.

.... **B.** to Boss Mommy, have power, defeat her.

.... **C.** to Counterhurt, get revenge, power with vengence.

.... **D.** to appear Disabled (get Mommy to think this).

To change the child's misbehavior Mother should:

.... **1.** Say nothing. Go for a walk with Father around the block.

.... **2.** Tell Jerry to leave the other kids alone and to mind his own business.

Answers: B, 1.

The child who feels responsible for the behavior of everyone else is functioning at Goal B. His purpose is to show his power and superiority over others. Very often he is an oldest child. Mother encourages this kind of behavior when she insists on his being responsible for everything that happens at home when she is gone. His worth becomes connected to directing and controlling other people. This is a heavy burden, for he grows older not wanting the younger children to grow up because, as they become more self-reliant and independent, his worth and value as a person becomes threatened, for they no longer depend on him. He therefore becomes past and rule oriented. Past oriented because it was in the past he was more responsible for his younger brothers and sisters and therefore felt more important. Rule oriented because rules have tended to protect his special position i.e., "Because you are the oldest you may . . ." His fondness for the past and for rules tend to generalize. Often the eldest is disrespectful of the rights of others, for he interferes, feeling responsible for all that goes on.

Mother should not make one child in the family responsible for the behavior of all the others, even though he be the oldest. This is especially true when the children are close in age. Each child should be responsible for his own behavior.

Sacrament Meeting Misbehavior

Four-year-old Joe is very active during church service. He hits and pokes his brothers and sisters, crawls under the benches, noisily stomps his feet, and when Mother pulls his ear to quiet him, he yells so that everyone looks Mother's way. Mother warns him before church and tells him during the service to be quiet, but he does not mind. Finally, Mother takes him to the nursery where he plays happily with the other children.

The child's goal is:

.... A. to get Attention, keep Mommy busy with him, get service.

.... B. to Boss Mommy, have power, defeat her.

.... C. to Counterhurt, get revenge, power with vengence.

.... D. to appear Disabled (get Mommy to think this).

To change the child's misbehavior Mother should:

.... 1. Give him a choice of settling down or sitting with her in the car. There she ignores him as she reads the Bible.

.... 2. Take him to the nursery room.

Answers: B, 1.

During sacrament service the child is in a powerful position to get Mother involved with him and then defeat her in a power struggle. Goals A and B are the typical misbehaving child's goals at this time. In the case of Joe it became a power struggle and he got Mother to do his bidding, take him to the nursery.

Public pressure works to the child's advantage and to Mother's disadvantage, for she, feeling the pressure from others, tends to give in to the child's demands, which reinforces his misbehavior.

It is best not to attempt to train the child when there are other people around. Mother is under too much pressure and the child is in a position to "work" the audience to his advantage and in the process defeat her.

Mother, however, can take steps to stop the misbehavior. One effective method is to withdraw with the child from the situation as was suggested in the case of Joe. In the car Joe can be obnoxious and it won't pay, for Mother ignores him. His misbehavior is not reinforced. He will soon prefer the association of others in sacrament meeting over the non-payoff situation in the car. Mother can take him back into the meeting when he agrees to behave in church. It may take several times before the child learns that if he misbehaves he will be taken to the car, but learn he will if Mother is consistent (her behavior is positively predictable to the child).

One note of caution is proposed. Often when Mother takes the misbehaving child out of the meeting, she introduces him to a much more pleasurable situation. This tends to reinforce the misbehavior. If he is taken out to play with playmates, given special food or attention through private little games with Mother, he will learn to misbehave for the purpose of getting Mother to take him to these pleasurable experiences.

Sexual Misbehavior

Mother had just moved into a new neighborhood. Jane, age four, and a neighbor boy, Bill, age five, were playing together in the back yard. Mother looked out and saw that both were naked from the waist down and Bill was putting his hands on Jane's genitals. Mother screamed, "Jane you get in the house this instant. Bill, you nasty boy, go home." Mother talked to other mothers in the neighborhood who had small daughters, and they remarked that Bill was doing such things all the time. They were all upset.

The child's goal is:

.... A. to get Attention, keep Mommy busy with him, get service.

.... B. to Boss Mommy, have power, defeat her.

.... C. to Counterhurt, get revenge, power with vengence.

.... D. to appear Disabled (get Mommy to think this).

To change the child's misbehavior Mother should:

.... 1. Tell Bill, because he is so nasty, he cannot play with Jane.

.... 2. Calmly say, "Jane, come help me make some pop corn. Bill, you have to leave now."

Answers: A, 2.

Sexual curiosity is natural; however, how Mother responds will help stimulate further sexual investigative behavior or decrease it. Sex can be used by the child to achieve special importance as in the case of Bill, or it can be used to defeat Mother through such behaviors as masturbating. Goals A and/or B are most often the goals of the child who habitually, sexually misbehaves.

When Mother sees her child sexually misbehaving with other children, she should calmly, but firmly, separate them. No retaliation should occur. Sexual curiosity is natural, but Mother's gentle, firm training will help the child to discipline himself so that he decreases such activity in the future. At the time of misbehavior, Mother should stop the activity with as little emotional interaction as possible and later, *when there is a good feeling between mother and child, talk with him about proper sexual conduct.*

Showing Off

Rodney delights in putting such things as mustard, ketchup, and horse radish, on his desserts. Mother tells him he is crazy, and the other kids laugh at him, but his "concoctions" get wilder.

The child's goal is:

.... **A.** to get Attention, keep Mommy busy with him, get service.

.... **B.** to Boss Mommy, have power, defeat her.

.... **C.** to Counterhurt, get revenge, power with vengence.

.... **D.** to appear Disabled (get Mommy to think this).

To change the child's misbehavior Mother should:

.... 1. Put the mustard, ketchup, and horse radish in the refrigerator and tell him he cannot eat like that.

.... 2. Continue quietly eating.

Answers: A, 2.

The "show-off" is striving for attention from others. His goal is A. The child is often stimulated by Mother to such behaviors by her habit of praising him in front of others for his rather useless, cute responses. If this continues, the child carries childlike behavior into adulthood where it is unacceptable generally. The child who continues to show-off is discouraged. He feels that to have a place with the family in cooperative, constructive ways is too difficult. He therefore resorts to showing off to put himself in the foreground. Very often the youngest child is the show-off in the family. He feels the competition is too stiff as he views his older brothers and sisters contributing in responsible ways; therefore, he chooses to make a place for himself as the clown.

Mother is to say nothing and do nothing when the child is showing off. She should not see his misbehavior. If attention is not drawn to him at such times, his misbehavior will diminish and cease, as there is no payoff. *He should be given an opportunity to contribute to the welfare of the family in responsible ways.*

Shyness

Four-year-old Susy is the youngest child. Whenever people come up to Mother at church, Susy picks up Mother's skirt and places it over her face or smilingly walks behind Mother.

The child's goal is:

.... A. to get Attention, keep Mommy busy with her, get service.

.... B. to Boss Mommy, have power, defeat her.

.... C. to Counterhurt, get revenge, power with vengence.

.... D. to appear Disabled (get Mommy to think this).

To change the child's misbehavior Mother should:

.... 1. Tell her friend she just doesn't know what to do with Susy for she is so shy.

.... 2. Say nothing about it. Continue talking with her friend.

Answers: A, 2.

The shy child is subtly able to get people involved with him. He strives for Goal A. Through his shyness he gains special attention or service from other people. This child is not the cowed, beaten down child who has given up and is striving for Goal D. The shy child forces others to get involved with him through his bashfulness and conspicuous doing nothing. He encourages much supervision from Mother and is expert at getting her to pay special attention to him. He demands special treatment by being easily embarrassed and reticent. Often when the shy child is approached he remains speechless, forcing others to work at getting him to interact with them. He is often a cute child.

Mother should refuse to play the shy-child's game by not getting involved with him when he acts shy and "cute." *She can encourage the child to more constructive and responsible behavior by giving him recognition for his cooperative endeavors while ignoring his manipulations for involvement and service.*

Sickness

Annette is ten. She has a very competent sister who is thirteen. Whenever Annette catches a cold, she complains of not feeling well for two or three weeks after all symptoms have apparently gone. Mother said, "Annette, it's your turn to do the dishes." Annette responded, "Mother, I just don't feel well. My head hurts. I have to rest." Ten minutes later she was watching TV.

The child's goal is:

.... **A.** to get Attention, keep Mommy busy with her, get service.

.... **B.** to Boss Mommy, have power, defeat her.

.... **C.** to Counterhurt, get revenge, power with vengence.

.... **D.** to appear Disabled (get Mommy to think this).

To change the child's misbehavior Mother should:

.... 1. Say, "If you're sick, you will have to go to bed and rest. No TV"

.... 2. Tell her she is lying and send her in to do the dishes.

Answers: B, 1.

Sickness may be used by the child to get his own way, Goal B. The over-solicitous, over-concerned mother generally stimulates the child to remain sickly. Treats and favors during sickness, such as malts, ice-cream floats, and pies and special TV privileges stimulate the child to use sickness as an excuse to get special service and avoid responsibility. He finds a special place of importance in the family by getting others to cater to him. When Mother makes a practice of giving special attention to the sick child, it often degenerates into the child demanding more and more service. Such a process is a power struggle. If the child feels that Mother has hurt him he may use sickness to demand so much of her that he hurts her physically and emotionally, Goal C. When Mother pampers and spoils the child during sickness the results are more sickness. The sick child needs only that care that is obsolutely necessary.

If the child is allowed to use sickness to avoid responsibility, he becomes irresponsible, develops low self-esteem, and tends to have poor relationships with others.

There is a problem of which Mother should be aware. Many times a mother who feels of little worth will semiconsciously strive to find her own importance by giving special service to the sick child. Then Mother's best interest dictates keeping the child ill. She pays off his manipulations for service and he rewards her by making her feel of value. They are soon locked into a poor relationship.

During sickness Mother should make sure she does not make things too pleasant for the child. She should avoid giving special privileges or foods except as they are necessary for his physical well-being. There should be nothing given to the child to tickle his palate or excite his pleasurable emotions. As soon as possible, the child should resume his normal activities. Mother can also use natural or logical consequences. For example, if the child comes home from school sick and later wants to go out in the evening to play, Mother is to say, "If you are too sick to go to school, you are too sick to play and must stay in the house to get well." There should be no unusual demonstrations of attention or affection during times of illness.

Speech Problems

Eleven-year-old Jody, a second child, stutters. Mother has told him to watch his speech and has corrected him each time she has observed him having difficulty. However, instead of getting better he seems to be getting worse.

The child's goal is:

.... A. to get Attention, keep Mommy busy with him, get service.

.... B. to Boss Mommy, have power, defeat her.

.... C. to Counterhurt, get revenge, power with vengence.

.... D. to appear Disabled (get Mommy to think this).

To change the child's misbehavior Mother should:

.... 1. Stop all TV privileges until he speaks better.

.... 2. Say nothing about his stuttering. Establish a relaxed relationship with him.

Answers: A, 2.

During the child's normal development he will exhibit irregularities in speech. Mother should not be concerned, for it's part of the process in learning to approximate good speech. Mistakes will be made. So called natural irregularities in speech become threatening to the child when Mother becomes over-concerned. He may then use his speech irregularities to get special attention, therefore, Goal A is the one for which the child with poor speech patterns most often strives.

When the child is learning to speak it is best to play down his mistakes. If Mother wants the child to learn to speak well, she should be a good model herself.

Stuttering

The child who stutters usually has demanding and perfectionistic parents. They expect much of him and put pressure on him to meet their expectations. Through stuttering the child gets special service and attention from others, Goal A, and also avoids responsibilities in his relationships. Stuttering may also be an expression of fear of failure, with overtones of rebellion and opposition, Goal B. Stuttering generally appears with the child when he is engaged in a relationship with people he fears. The child who stutters often has a great desire to please.

Stuttering should be ignored. Be calm with the stuttering child in all your responses. Make sure there is no tension between you and the child as you interact. Your relationships with the child should be friendly and peaceful. There should be no undue demands placed on him and attention should not be given to his stuttering.

Psuedo Deaf Mute

There are children who act as if they are deaf mutes but in reality are not. Generally, it is found that family members give into the every whim of the child who is pseudo deaf. They communicate to him on his ground, using his special language. Usually he is pampered, indulged, and spoiled. Every body movement this child uses, every grunt and groan, produces quick responses from a very sensitive mother who reinforces the "deafness" with the special communicative relationship.

Mother should ignore the child's foreign language. She should respond only to those verbal cues that have common meaning. It is often found that when Mother stops communicating to him in the old ways he becomes upset and angered and throws tantrums. He should be ignored at this time also. Mother is to be firm with herself and not give in to his demands by regressing to the old ways. This child is to be understood only when he speaks verbally.

Baby Talk

The child who talks "baby talk" builds a unique relationship with Mother. It gets him special involvement, Goal A, with her. No other child in the family has such a unique position. Where no physical disability is discovered, it may be assumed that the child is using "baby talk" for the payoff he receives.

To help the child, Mother should disengage from him when he uses such speech. He will improve his speech habits only when it is beneficial for him to do so. As long as Mother talks baby talk with him he will continue to use it. When Mother refuses to be engaged with him at that level, he will soon drop it, for there is no longer any payoff.

Stalling

The family is always ready on time for Sunday School, except for twelve-year-old Melinda. This morning was typical. Everyone was ready and waiting. Mother called, "Let's go, Melinda." She called back, "Just a minute mother, I'm not quite ready." Ten minutes later Mother had called four more times, but the family was still waiting.

The child's goal is:

.... A. to get Attention, keep Mommy busy with her, get service.

.... B. to Boss Mommy, have power, defeat her.

.... C. to Counterhurt, get revenge, power with vengence.

.... D. to appear Disabled (get Mommy to think this).

To change the child's misbehavior Mother should:

.... 1. Bring her out with force if necessary.

.... 2. Say nothing more. Leave at the appointed time with or without her.

Answers: A, 2.

Melinda's goal is to prove her importance by getting everyone in the family to wait for her. She also gets much involvement with Mother who keeps telling her to hurry.

Stalling is used by the typical child to keep Mother busy with him. Therefore, Goal A is the goal of the child who stalls. Mother should refuse to get involved with the stalling child. She should not nag him as this is his payoff.

Let the child experience the logical consequences of his stalling. For example, if he stalls when he should be eating, Mother quietly but surely picks up all plates when everyone else is finished, scrapes off the food, and starts the dishes. If, rather than getting ready for school, he "fiddles around," Mother does nothing to interfere with his experiencing the consequences of being late. This includes *not* going to his rescue when the school takes action. In this way the child will learn from the consequences of his *own* actions.

Stealing

Ten-year-old Bill bought a $4.00 model car with $5.00 he took from Mother's purse without her knowledge. Mother cried, then spanked him when she found out about it.

The child's goal is:

.... A. to get Attention, keep Mommy busy with him, get service.

.... B. to Boss Mommy, have power, defeat her.

.... C. to Counterhurt, get revenge, power with vengence.

.... D. to appear Disabled (get Mommy to think this).

To change the child's misbehavior Mother should:

.... 1. Spank him harder and tell him how disappointed you are in him.

.... 2. Show no hurt in facial expression or tone of voice. Say calmly, "What can we arrange for you to do to repay the $5.00?"

Answers: C, 2.

The child who steals is striving for Goal C. His purpose in his stealing is to hurt back. He wants revenge. The child is usually very discouraged and is communicating through his stealing that he wants to hurt others as he feels they have hurt him. He hurts and is hurting back. Because he believes people treat him unfairly, he feels that he is not loved or accepted.

There is also an element of attention getting in stealing. He wants to get Mother to pay him special attention. Many children steal awkwardly in order to get caught to draw attention to themselves. Stealing, therefore, often serves a double purpose, that of hurting Mother and forcing her to give special attention, usually in a very emotional atmosphere.

The typical reaction to one who steals generally reinforces his misbehavior. The tendency is to respond in a horrified and concerned manner. This makes the child who has stolen very special and shows Mother's hurt. His expectations in stealing are met. He is taught that stealing is an effective way of achieving his goals.

Among other things, Mother should respond by treating such a child calmly. Any emotional expression would increase his chances of getting payoff. The child should experience the logical consequences of his behavior. He should make restitution for that which he has taken. This is to be arranged if he is unable to replace it.

There is another danger in Mother's getting emotionally upset when the child steals. She may treat the child like a criminal and say such things as "I'll never be able to trust you again." This communicates that Mother expects him to be a thief in the future. Children tend to meet the expectations of their parents. He will verbalize to himself, "If Mother believes I am that way, I guess I must be," and he has an excuse for behaving irresponsibly in the future.

Mother is to look at the total picture and realize how the child feels about his belonging in the family. Maybe he is saying that his only pathway to importance is to do something special even if it is negative, such as stealing. Or he may be saying, "I'm hurting you as you have hurt me."

The secret in dealing with the child who steals is to be calm, casual and firm. He should make restitution for the thing which he has stolen. At a time when there is a good relationship, the consequences of stealing can be discussed with him. Mother should continue to have faith and trust in him. *Mother should help the child to feel he is worthwhile and important by getting involved with him in constructive, cooperative ways when he is not demanding her involvement.*

Stubbornness

Mother told Alex to hurry up and eat so that he would have time to empty the waste baskets before he went to school. Alex said nothing but continued eating. Mother said, "Do you hear me?" Alex' response was, "Yeah." When he finished eating he went into the bedroom and slammed the door. Five minutes later Mother shouted, "You get out here right now and empty those waste baskets." Alex shouted back, "I don't have time."

The child's goal is:

----------- A.   to get Attention, keep Mommy busy with him, get service.

----------- B.   to Boss Mommy, have power, defeat her.

----------- C.   to Counterhurt, get revenge, power with vengence.

----------- D.   to appear Disabled (get Mommy to think this).

To change the child's misbehavior Mother should:

----------- 1.   Say nothing until he leaves for school. If the waste baskets are not emptied by then say, "Alex, you'll have to finish your work before you go."

----------- 2.   Tell Alex he cannot play with his friends that night.

Answers: B, 1.

The stubborn child is a powerful child. His goal is to be boss, to prove his control and power over other people. He is often subtly disobedient. The goal of this child is to get Mother to quarrel with him so he can defeat her. Mother's first impulse is to get angry with him and tell him that he cannot get away with it. This will tend to pay off the child and stimulate power struggles in the future.

The suggested procedure is for Mother to leave the child alone. Refuse to become engaged with the child in conflicts. Then improve your relationships with him by having enjoyable times together when he is not angry. Help him to feel that his place is secure with you. You may also watch your demands and control of the child. It is often found that the child who develops a pattern of stubbornness is the product of a demanding and stubborn mother.

When the child refuses to cooperate in the upkeep of the home, as in the case of Alex, it proves very helpful to give the child a choice of either cooperating with Mother or of doing for himself. If he chooses not to cooperate, the logical consequences are that Mother no longer cooperates with him and the child does such things for himself as washing and ironing his own clothes or they do not get done. This disengages Mother from nagging him to do things for her and enables the child to experience the logical results of noncooperation. Cooperation is a two-way street. The sooner this is learned the better prepared he will be to face life.

Stupidity

Ten-year-old Jerry never seems to do anything. Mother asked him to go to Aunt Martha's five blocks away, for the purpose of picking up a button holer Mother had arranged to borrow. Jerry insisted he did not know the way even though he had been there many times before with the family. He said he was not going.

The child's goal is:

----------- A. to get Attention, keep Mommy busy with him, get service.

----------- B. to Boss Mommy, have power, defeat her.

----------- C. to Counterhurt, get revenge, power with vengence.

----------- D. to appear Disabled (get Mommy to think this).

To change the child's misbehavior Mother should:

----------- 1. Say: "Well I guess I'll have to go then."

----------- 2. Say: "I'm sure you can find the way."

Answers: B, 2.

The child who hides behind a mask of stupidity is a powerful child. He is operating at level "B". He who hides behind this mask is often found to be pampered and spoiled. He gets Mother to do everything for him. This child, when he is put in school or starts playing with playmates, finds that he cannot keep up. Due to his ability to manipulate Mother to do things for him, he has not developed. He quickly becomes discouraged. He believes he is stupid and gets others to believe this also. The child may go to great lengths to prove his stupidity in order to avoid responsibility. One of the problems of the past has been that the I.Q. scores on these children have tended to support these misconceptions about them so that teachers as well as parents have low expectations for them.

Mother should not scold, ridicule, or compare this child with others. She is to let him experience the consequences of his behavior. Too often Mother is the one who experiences the consequences of his misbehavior. For example, when the child fails in school, Mother is often more upset than the child. If the child feels that Mother is more interested in his success in school than he, he is given an excellent tool for defeating her.

Mother can stimulate the interests of this child more naturally by taking the child on field trips, to museums, zoos, farms, and so on. She may also introduce him to good books. In order to stimulate him to desire knowledge and appreciate work, the atmosphere in the home should be one of pleasure and enthusiasm.

Thumb-Sucking

Jody, age three, sucks his thumb almost continuously, or so it seems to Mother. While Mother was visiting a friend, Jody put his thumb in his mouth. Mother took it out as soon as she saw it. Jody soon had it back in. Mother took it out. In five minutes Jody had it back in. Embarrassed, Mother said, "For Heaven's sake, Jody, quit sucking your thumb."

The child's goal is:

-----------   A.   to get Attention, keep Mommy busy with him, get service.

-----------   B.   to Boss Mommy, have power, defeat her.

-----------   C.   to Counterhurt, get revenge, power with vengence.

-----------   D.   to appear Disabled (get Mommy to think this).

To change the child's misbehavior Mother should:

-----------   1.   Say nothing, keep on talking to her friend.

-----------   2.   Say, "If you can't stop sucking your thumb you'll have to play outdoors."

Answers: A, 1.

Getting attention or defeating Mother are the goals of the child who habitually sucks his thumb. Many young children go through a period when they put their thumbs in their mouths. This is usually not a problem until Mother becomes concerned and starts nagging. The more Mother nags, the more he will tend to suck his thumb. Mother's nagging is a reward of special concern. The child may try to defeat her by completely ignoring her requests and demands to stop if she becomes too demanding. A sure way to ingrain the habit of thumb-sucking is for Mother to take special pains to get him to stop.

The suggested procedure is for Mother to say nothing and do nothing that will give the child attention for sucking his thumb. She can, however, distract his attention to other things that involve him to the extent that thumb-sucking is impractical for him. He cannot very well suck his thumb if he is working with clay. If Mother ignores the thumb-sucking, peer pressure will take care of the situation as the child gets older. Mother can also encourage the child to become active in many different kinds of interesting things in life. This will help him feel better towards himself about his place in the family, and he will have less need to keep Mother involved.

Temper Tantrums

Five-year-old Sandra was playing at the neighbors. Mother called her to come home. She continued playing. Mother went to where she was playing and told her to come home immediately. She continued playing. Mother grabbed her by the hand and started pulling her toward home. Sandra started screaming and yelling at the top of her lungs. She also began kicking at Mother.

The child's goal is:

.... A. to get Attention, keep Mommy busy with her, get service.

.... B. to Boss Mommy, have power, defeat her.

.... C. to Counterhurt, get revenge, power with vengence.

.... D. to appear Disabled (get Mommy to think this).

To change the child's misbehavior Mother should:

.... 1. Stop and paddle her.

.... 2. Give her the choice of walking or being carried.

Answers: B, 2.

To show Mother who is boss, Goal B, is the goal of the child who throws temper tantrums. This is his way of showing his power and ability to defeat Mother. His degree of worth becomes equated with his degree of power. The child who develops patterns of throwing temper tantrums is usually a spoiled, indulged child who is used to getting his own way. He throws temper tantrums in order to scare Mother into giving in to his demands. This child is unsure of his own worth, self-esteem, and place with others. He mistakenly strives to achieve them through power.

The procedure which Mother is to use with this child is to ignore his demands and not allow herself to get engaged in the temper tantrums. She should be calm and firm with herself, firm in the sense that she does not allow herself to be drawn into the situation. When the child throws a temper tantrum, Mother is to do such things as go to another room or the bathroom and lock herself in with a good book and radio. She comes out when she is finished reading and the child has settled down. She should have the confidence in herself that she can handle the situation which will be sensed by the child. He tends not to test the confident mother too long.

If the child becomes destructive in his temper tantrums, Mother is to arrange the environment in such a manner that he can do little damage. He may also be given a choice of settling down or going to the time-out room. This is to be done in a firm but gentle manner with a tone of voice that shows no anger or emotional upset. *At other times Mother should work to establish a more friendly relationship with the child and encourage him to greater self-reliance.*

Vanity

Jan is a beautiful twelve-year-old. Each evening Mother, among other things, brushes her daughter's hair until it shines. When Mother says she is too busy, Jane responds with, "Mother, only you can make my hair look so beautiful."

The child's goal is:

.... A. to get Attention, keep Mommy busy with her, get service.

.... B. to Boss Mommy, have power, defeat her.

.... C. to Counterhurt, get revenge, power with vengence.

.... D. to appear Disabled (get Mommy to think this).

To change the child's misbehavior Mother should:

.... 1. Tell her to get Collette to do it for her.

.... 2. Say, "I'm sure you can learn Jane." Then go about your work.

Answers: A, 2.

Vanity is a more subtle way the child has of getting special attention from Mother. The goal is A. If the child is praised by Mother for what he is rather than for what he has achieved or can achieve, vanity is stimulated. The vain child has been able to get others interested and involved with him without doing anything constructive. He gets attention for simply being beautiful or good-looking. He is stimulated to vanity by Mother's praise of his beauty. If he perceives that his place in the family is based on his beauty, he will tend to become vain. The danger is that beauty can be easily marred. The vain child is usually quite dependent. He is not able to do many things well. He is a noncontributor. He therefore has feelings of inferiority and of low self-esteem which contribute to his insecurity.

It is also suggested that the child who is extremely sloppy in his dress and appearance is vain. This child is trying to impress others through sloppiness, not neatness.

It is recommended that Mother play down the vain child's dress and good looks. She can, however, set a neat example herself. One thing working against this child is the ease with which he is able to get praise and involvement from others through his good looks for it takes effort to get recognition through good works, responsible behavior, and worthwhile contributions to the family. Mother should do all she can to stimulate the self-reliance and independence of the child.

The Chronically Weak

Ten-year-old Jill talks in a high thin voice. Mother hesitates to ask Jill to do anything for fear it will overtax her. This morning Jill got up and seemed to be in good spirits. Mother said, "Jill, please make your bed and clean up your room today as I don't think I'll have time to do it myself." At breakfast, Jill said she didn't feel very well and stretched out on the sofa with her eyes closed. Medical doctors can find nothing wrong with her.

The child's goal is:

.... A. to get Attention, keep Mommy busy with her, get service.

.... B. to Boss Mommy, have power, defeat her.

.... C. to Counterhurt, get revenge, power with vengence.

.... D. to appear Disabled (get Mommy to think this).

To change the child's misbehavior Mother should:

.... 1. Put her to bed.

.... 2. Say nothing now. When she starts to watch TV say, "After you have made your bed and cleaned up your room you may watch TV"

Answers: B, 2.

The child who is chronically weak or unable is subtly striving for Goal B. His is a devious and powerful method of avoiding responsibility and getting other people to do things for him. Mother will usually excuse the chronically weak child by referring to his emotional or physical states as being reasons why he cannot accept responsibility. Because the child is seldom physically weak Mother's over concern is a mistake. The child has simply learned to use weakness as a means of getting special service from other people or getting others in his power. Often he has had a period of sickness in his life, such as rheumatic fever, where he experienced being pampered and the "pleasures" of avoiding responsibility. Many professional people feed into this child by diagnosing him as a weak child. It is suggested that unless the evidence of organic weakness is sure, Mother not accept the child's excuses.

The danger with this child is that as he gets special services from others he does not develop himself. He avoids responsibility and does not develop self-reliance and independence. He therefore feels worthless and no good and continues to demand more and more service in order to feel better. This child often becomes a tyrant of both Mother and professionals.

It is suggested that Mother not pamper him. He is not to be given any special consideration or privileges over any of the other children. He should be encouraged to work along with Mother and the rest of the family. His constructive contributions to the welfare of the family should be acknowledged. *Every effort should be made to encourage self-reliance and independence. Care should be taken by Mother to ignore his assumed weaknesses.*

Water Power

Eight-year-old Sandra seems to cry very easily. Mother asked her to hurry up and finish sweeping the floor so she could get it waxed. Sandra began to cry. Big tears rolled down her cheeks and her shoulders began to heave. Mother stopped washing the dishes, took the broom, and finished sweeping the floor.

The child's goal is:

.... A. to get Attention, keep Mommy busy with her, get service.

.... B. to Boss Mommy, have power, defeat her.

.... C. to Counterhurt, get revenge, power with vengence.

.... D. to appear Disabled (get Mommy to think this).

To change the child's misbehavior Mother should:

.... 1. Send her to bed to rest.

.... 2. Say nothing. Continue washing the dishes.

Answers: B, 2.

One of the most effective ways the child has of forcing Mother to do his bidding, Goal B, is to cry. The child may use tears to avoid the responsibility of facing up to his own misbehavior, to avoid contributing responsibility, or to get others to wait on him.

The child who develops the habit of crying is discouraged about his own ability to contribute to the family as well as others or about his ability to get involved in constructive ways. He may feel threatened by the attention Mother is giving to a younger brother or sister. He may also feel he cannot compete with an older brother or sister and therefore resorts to crying. Crying is a subtle, unconstuctive, powerful method the child has of getting others to give in to his demands.

Generally, Mother should say nothing and have no interaction with the child when he cries to avoid responsibility or to get special consideration. Walking into another room or continuing what you are doing are effective ways of not feeding into and reinforcing his crying.

Mother should realize that the child is discouraged and, at times when he is not demanding it, she should have experiences with him which build his courage to participate in mutually respectful relationships.

Some Additional Practice Cases

These cases are presented to help Mother gain greater proficiency in applying the principles for correcting the misbehavior of the disturbing child. Opportunity is also provided for practice in encouraging the child to good behavior at a time other than when he is misbehaving.

The Case of Jim

Five-year-old Jim is an only child. His mother works; therefore, he goes to a nursery. Invariably, as soon as mother picks up Jim after work he demands that she give him gum and candy. When mother refuses to give into his demands he starts to scream, cry, and say to her that she doesn't love him.

The child's goal is:

.... A. to get Attention

.... B. to be Boss

.... C. to Counterhurt (get revenge)

.... D. to appear Disabled (wants you to assume this).

To change the child's misbehavior Mother should:

.... 1. Stop the car and get some candy.

.... 2. Tell Jim to shut up until they get home.

.... 3. Stop the car until Jim quiets down.

To encourage good behavior Mother should:

.... a. Get out of the car and meet Jimmy with a hug and a smile.

.... b. Spank him and put him to bed when they get home.

.... c. Tell him she will bake him a chocolate cake if he will be quiet.

Answers: C, 3, a.

The Case of Johnny

John, a four-year-old, is the youngest child and the only boy in his family. He has two older sisters, ages five and six. John throws himself on the floor, kicks his legs, and screams when Mother doesn't give him what he wants.

The child's goal is:

.... A. to get Attention

.... B. to be Boss

.... C. to Counterhurt (get revenge)

.... D. to appear Disabled (wants you to assume this).

To change the child's misbehavior Mother should:

.... 1. Pick up the child and cuddle him.

.... 2. Show no emotion and walk into another room.

.... 3. Tell the child that in this home we do not allow temper tantrums.

To encourage good behavior Mother should:

.... a. Let him help set the table.

.... b. Spank him each time he has a tantrum.

.... c. Tell his Father about his bad misbehavior.

Answers: B, 2, a.

The Case of Jane

Jane is eleven. She has two younger brothers, ages nine and six. Last night when the family was visiting friends, Jane kept returning to where the adults were. She continually interrupted with such words as, "I want more to eat. I am freezing to death. The other kids are being mean to me." This is typical of her behavior when visiting.

The child's goal is:

.... A. to get Attention

.... B. to be Boss

.... C. to Counterhurt (get revenge)

.... D. to appear Disabled (wants you to assume this).

To change the child's misbehavior Mother should:

.... 1. Tell Jane she is rude to interrupt and send her back to play with the other children.

.... 2. Ignore her remarks but talk to her at bedtime.

.... 3. Send her out to the car.

To encourage good behavior Mother should:

.... a. Immediately go to her and put her arm around her.

.... b. Go to her some other time, put her arms around her and talk with her about things both enjoy.

.... c. Have her sit on her lap.

Answers: A, 2, b.

The Case of Tom

Tom has two older sisters, ages six and five. He is four. Tom talks continually during meals and eats very little. Mother tells him over and over to hurry up, but he does not respond. It ends when Mother feeds him.

The child's goal is:

....   A. to get Attention

....   B. to be Boss

....   C. to Counterhurt (get revenge)

....   D. to appear Disabled (wants you to assume this).

To change the child's misbehavior Mother should:

....   1. Stop feeding him.

....   2. When everyone else is through, quietly pick up Tom's plate along with the rest and scrape the food down the garbage disposal.

....   3. Send him to bed if he doesn't eat.

To encourage good behavior Mother should:

....   a. Provide small helpings, no snacks between meals.

....   b. Continue to feed him.

....   c. Refuse to talk to him at mealtime.

Answers: A, 1 & 2, a.

The Case of Jane and Bob

Jane is ten and Bob is nine. They fight almost constantly or so it seems to Mother. She tries to help them solve their difficulties.

The children's goal is:

....   **A.**   to get Attention

....   **B.**   to be Boss

....   **C.**   to Counterhurt (get revenge)

....   **D.**   to appear Disabled (wants you to assume this).

To change the children's misbehavior Mother should:

....   **1.**   Find out who is to blame and send him/ her to the basement.

....   **2.**   Stay out of their quarrels and fights.

....   **3.**   Spank them both.

To encourage good behavior Mother should:

....   **a.**   Tell them she has confidence in their ability to work out their differences without Mother's help.

....   **b.**   Agree to bake them a cake if they will promise to stop quarreling so often.

....   **c.**   Tell them their Heavenly Father doesn't like kids who fight.

Answers: A, 2, a.

The Case of Dan

Dan is four. He has a brother, Ray, who is seven months old. Dan keeps asking his mother for things throughout the day. He will say, "I want my milk. Get my shoes. Get me a drink of water." Mother gets tired and angry. She finds herself yelling at him. When she doesn't do what he wants, he screams and kicks the furniture.

The child's goal is:

.... A. to get Attention

.... B. to be Boss

.... C. to Counterhurt (get revenge)

.... D. to appear Disabled (wants you to assume this).

To change the child's misbehavior Mother should:

.... 1. Send him to his room.

.... 2. Spank him and send him to his room.

.... 3. Ignore his demands, say nothing, do nothing.

To encourage good behavior Mother should:

.... a. Suggest to him that he is too big to act that way.

.... b. Let him help dress and feed his little brother.

.... c. Tell him he must set a good example for Ray.

Answers: B, 3, b.

The Case of Bill

Bill, an only child, is seven years old. Whenever he plays outside and gets hurt by the neighborhood kids, he goes running and crying to Mother. Mother has told his playmates in the past to be careful with him, but it does not seem to help. He still gets hurt and comes crying several times a day to Mother.

The child's goal is:

.... A. to get Attention

.... B. to be Boss

.... C. to Counterhurt (get revenge)

.... D. to appear Disabled (wants you to assume this).

To change the child's misbehavior Mother should:

.... 1. Take better care of Bill.

.... 2. Change his playmates.

.... 3. Tell him you are sure he can work it out with his friends.

To encourage good behavior Mother should:

.... a. Respond quietly and calmly to him, encouraging him to solve his own difficulties. Encourage him to do more things on his own.

.... b. Love him when he is hurt.

.... c. Do more things for him.

Answers: A, 3, a.

The Case of Jane

Jane is eight. She has two sisters, ages four and two. Last night she said to Mother, "Why don't you make me a dress like Sue's mother made for her. Sue's mother loves her." At another time last night she said, "Why don't you have time to do my hair like you used to? You don't have time for me anymore."

The child's goal is:

.... A. to get Attention

.... B. to be Boss

.... C. to Counterhurt (get revenge)

.... D. to appear Disabled (wants you to assume this).

To change the child's misbehavior Mother should:

.... 1. Tell Jane she should be grateful Mother spends as much time as she does for her.

.... 2. Show neither hurt nor concern, in words, tone of voice, facial expression nor posture.

.... 3. Go to her, hug her, and tell her how much she loves her.

To encourage good behavior Mother should:

.... a. Let her help make out a grocery list, then go shopping together.

.... b. Make a dress like Sue's.

.... c. Tell her how happy she should be to be in the family.

Answers: C, 2, a.

The Case of Rod

Rod is second in a family of four boys. Reed, the oldest, is good in athletics, gets high grades in school, and does his chores well at home. Rod does not do well in school, is clumsy, refuses to get involved in sports, and is sloppy in doing his chores. He looks sad much of the time.

The child's goal is:

.... A. to get Attention

.... B. to be Boss

.... C. to Counterhurt (get revenge)

.... D. to appear Disabled (wants you to assume this).

To change the child's misbehavior Mother should:

.... 1. Show Rod where he is failing and get him to straighten up.

.... 2. Ignore his bad habits and emphasize the strengths he has.

.... 3. Suggest that he follow Rod's example.

To encourage good behavior Mother should:

.... a. Compare Rod to relatives she admires.

.... b. Have expectations for him that he feels are achievable.

.... c. Never compare him with others. Emphasize his own unique talents or skills.

Answers: D, 2, b & c.

The Case of Diane

Diane, age seven, is an only child. Mother is continually after her for one reason or another. Diane's clothes are never kept as clean as Mother would like nor does she ever do her chores as well as Mother would like. Recently Diane has started to masturbate. Mother has scolded, yelled at her, and spanked her. Diane says she is sorry, but she continues.

The child's goal is:

.... A. to get Attention

.... B. to be Boss

.... C. to Counterhurt (get revenge)

.... D. to appear Disabled (wants you to assume this).

To change the child's misbehavior Mother should:

.... 1. Not see the mastubation. You are to ignore it.

.... 2. Spank harder.

.... 3. Tell her you are disappointed in her.

To encourage good behavior Mother should:

.... a. Never criticize her work. Have enjoyable times together.

.... b. Avoid ordering her to do things. Provide choices for her.

.... c. Be stricter with her.

Answers: B, 1, a & b.

The Case of Lydia

Lydia, age six, is the youngest. She has one older brother and one older sister. Recently she had the flu. She seems well but refuses to eat what the others eat. Her typical response is, "That makes my stomach ache." Mother has bought her malts, ice cream and made floats for her during the past week. The medical doctor says there is nothing wrong with her. She still refuses to get out of bed most of the day and, therefore, is served in bed.

The child's goal is:

.... A. to get Attention

.... B. to be Boss

.... C. to Counterhurt (get revenge)

.... D. to appear Disabled (wants you to assume this).

To change the child's misbehavior Mother should:

.... 1. Continue to do as she has done.

.... 2. Read her stories in bed.

.... 3. Set a place for her. If she does not come to the table to eat she gets nothing until the next meal.

To encourage good behavior Mother should:

.... a. Tell her how hard she is making it for Mother.

.... b. Do nothing for her that she can do for herself.

.... c. Use phrases like, "I am sure you can do it," and "Practice makes things easier."

Answers: B, 3, b & c.

The Case of Joan

Joan is eight. She has two older brothers in high school. Joan is late getting up in the mornings on the average of twice a week. Mother therefore drives her to school so she will not get a tardy slip.

The child's goal is:

.... A. to get Attention

.... B. to be Boss

.... C. to Counterhurt (get revenge)

.... D. to appear Disabled (wants you to assume this).

To change the child's misbehavior Mother should:

.... 1. Wake her earlier.

.... 2. Have Joan get an alarm clock.

.... 3. Not drive her to school.

To encourage good behavior Mother should:

.... a. Let her suffer the consequences of being late for school.

.... b. Call her more often.

.... c. Have her father discipline her.

Answers: A, 2 & 3, a.

The Case of Jerry

Jerry is three. He has two older brothers, ages seven and nine. He is crying and hitting his head against the floor.

The child's goal is:

.... A. to get Attention

.... B. to be Boss

.... C. to Counterhurt (get revenge)

.... D. to appear Disabled (wants you to assume this).

To change the child's misbehavior Mother should:

.... 1. Continue washing the dishes.

.... 2. Pick him up and cuddle him.

.... 3. Tell him to stop it.

To encourage good behavior Mother should:

.... a. Let him help dry the dishes at other times.

.... b. Tell his father about his misbehaviors.

.... c. Point out to Jerry other kids who are having tantrums and show him how silly they look.

Answers: B, 1, a.

The Case of Darrell

Darrell who is five usually has his shirt on backwards when he comes down for breakfast. Mother has to tell him almost every morning to put it on right.

The child's goal is:

....   A. to get Attention

....   B. to be Boss

....   C. to Counterhurt (get revenge)

....   D. to appear Disabled (wants you to assume this).

To change the child's misbehavior Mother should:

....   1. Tell him he is sharp enough to know how it should go.

....   2. Send him from the table.

....   3. Say nothing, do nothing, see nothing.

To encourage good behavior Mother should:

....   a. Help him to dress more often

....   b. Let him help dress Jane who is two.

....   c. Have the older children help him dress.

The Case of Sheryl

Mother is on the telephone. Sheryl who is three gets in the flour bin and pours some flour on the floor.

The child's goal is:

....   A.   to get Attention

....   B.   to be Boss

....   C.   to Counterhurt (get revenge)

....   D.   to appear Disabled (wants you to assume this).

To change the child's misbehavior Mother should:

....   1.   Hang up quickly before she makes a mess.

....   2.   Appear not to see the situation.

....   3.   Yell at her to stop it.

To encourage good behavior Mother should:

....   a.   Let Sheryl help her make rolls.

....   b.   Spank her each time she is naughty.

....   c.   Send her to her room.

Answers: A, 2, a.

The Case of Bobby

Bobby is six. He likes to play with his friends and is usually late for supper. Mother keeps going to the door and calling him.

The child's goal is:

.... A. to get Attention

.... B. to be Boss

.... C. to Counterhurt (get revenge)

.... D. to appear Disabled (wants you to assume this).

To change the child's misbehavior Mother should:

.... 1. Serve supper promptly on schedule.

.... 2. Go get him.

.... 3. Call him earlier.

To encourage good behavior Mother should:

.... a. Serve his favorite foods.

.... b. Use colors he likes best on the table.

.... c. If he is late, he prepares his own food or goes without supper.

Answers: A, 1, c.

The Case of Terry

Terry said he couldn't do his chores because he felt both tired and dizzy. He stayed up and watched TV. This often happens. He always seems too sick to do his work, but seems OK while watching TV.

The child's goal is:

- .... A. to get Attention
- .... B. to be Boss
- .... C. to Counterhurt (get revenge)
- .... D. to appear Disabled (wants you to assume this).

To change the child's misbehavior Mother should:

- .... 1. Make sure he eats well and gets plenty of sleep.
- .... 2. No chores, no TV.
- .... 3. Make the house more comfortable for him.

To encourage good behavior Mother should:

- .... a. Give no special privileges when he is sick.
- .... b. Have him do more chores when he claims he is sick.
- .... c. Tell him his older brother doesn't act that way.

Answers B, 2, a.

The Case of Jean

Jean who is five is playing with her seven year old brother, Joe. Jean comes crying to Mother saying that Joe will not let her play with his ball. Big tears roll down her cheeks and her shoulders shake.

The child's goal is:

.... A. to get Attention

.... B. to be Boss

.... C. to Counterhurt (get revenge)

.... D. to appear Disabled (wants you to assume this).

To change the child's misbehavior Mother should:

.... 1. Go to Joe and insist he share.

.... 2. Say to Jean, "The two of you can work it through."

.... 3. Give Jean a piece of cake and a glass of milk.

To encourage good behavior Mother should:

.... a. Force them both to experience sharing.

.... b. Stay out of their quarrels.

.... c. Practice sharing some of her things with both Jean and Joe.

Answers: B, 2, b & c.

The Case of Barbara

Barbara who is eleven smiles continually. She is always very agreeable. Today she spent thirty minutes in front of the mirror looking this way and that. She said to her mother, "Don't you think I am pretty today?" This is one of her favorite questions.

The child's goal is:

- .... A. to get Attention
- .... B. to be Boss
- .... C. to Counterhurt (get revenge)
- .... D. to appear Disabled (wants you to assume this).

To change the child's misbehavior Mother should:

- .... 1. Tell her she is vain and too proud.
- .... 2. Ignore her physical beauty. Avoid referring to it.
- .... 3. Fuss over her more. Comb her hair for her.

To encourage good behavior Mother should:

- .... a. Show her how physical beauty can be a handicap.
- .... b. Praise her constructive acts.
- .... c. Tell her how awful she looks in the mornings.

Answers: A, 2, b.

The Case of Harry

Harry is ten. He has two younger brothers and one younger sister. His favorite expressions during the day include such statements as, "Mother, Joe and Bill are fighting again. Jane's messing up the living room."

The child's goal is:

.... A. to get Attention

.... B. to be Boss

.... C. to Counterhurt (get revenge)

.... D. to appear Disabled (wants you to assume this).

To change the child's misbehavior Mother should:

.... 1. Tell him to mind his business.

.... 2. Praise him for being a good boy.

.... 3. Say, "They can work it out," and "That's Jane's business."

To encourage good behavior Mother should:

.... a. Give Harry responsibility for hosing down the carport. Recognize his good work and effort.

.... b. Praise him for watching his brothers and sister so closely.

.... c. Encourage him to get a newspaper delivery route.

Answers: A, 3, a & c.

The Case of Mary

Mary, age eleven, wanted a new dress for her birthday party. Mother felt the family could not afford it. Mary said, "You are unfair. You always buy things you want, but never things I want."

The child's goal is:

....   A.   to get Attention

....   B.   to be Boss

....   C.   to Counterhurt (get revenge)

....   D.   to appear Disabled (wants you to assume this).

To change the child's misbehavior Mother should:

....   1.   Say to her "How can you be so cruel and thoughtless."

....   2.   Say, "You may be right." Mother shows no hurt.

....   3.   Show her how much she has in comparison to the people of India.

To encourage good behavior Mother should:

....   a.   Let her plan her own birthday party.

....   b.   Tell her how poor the people are down the street.

....   c.   Let her help plan the meals. Then, take her grocery shopping.

Answers: C, 2, a & c.

The Case of Mark

Father died six months ago leaving Mother with Mark, age five, and Annette, age three. Mother told Mark he would have to turn off the TV as it was time for bed. Mark said, "If Dad were here he would let us watch as long as we want."

The child's goal is:

    ....   A. to get Attention

    ....   B. to be Boss

    ....   C. to Counterhurt (get revenge)

    ....   D. to appear Disabled (wants you to assume this).

To change the child's misbehavior Mother should:

    ....   1. Go over and turn off the TV immediately.

    ....   2. Say to Mark, "How can you talk that way."

    ....   3. Say, "It's possible," then give him the choice of turning off the TV himself or having Mother do it.

To encourage good behavior Mother should:

    ....   a. Have a set time for watching TV and stick to it.

    ....   b. Let them watch when they want to.

    ....   c. Tell him how disappointed Dad would be with him when he doesn't do what Mother says.

Answers: C, 3, a.

Misbehavior in Series—Mother Follows Through Sue ("Bugging Mommy")

Episode 1

While Mother was ironing, Sue kept coming up to her and jerking off the ironing board that article of clothing being pressed.

To correct the misbehavior Mother should:

....   a. Slap her hand.

...✓...   b. Say, "Would you like to settle down or would you like to leave the room?"

Answer: b

Episode 2

Sue continued to pull the clothing off the ironing board.

To correct the misbehavior Mother should:

...✓...   a. Put her outside the room and shut the door.

....   b. Ask her if she would like to leave.

Answer: a

Episode 3

Sue immediately opened the door and walked back into the room.

To correct the misbehavior Mother should:

....   a. Put her out again.

...✓...   b. Say, "You'll have to stay out or go to the time-out room."

Answer: b

Episode 4

Sue stayed in the room. She would not go out.

To correct the misbehavior Mother should:

.......✓....... a. Take her to the time-out room.

.... b. Give her another chance as she's stopped taking the clothes off the ironing board.

Answer: a

Bob (disobeys)

Episode 1

The family has agreed that all chores are to be done before TV can be watched. Tonight, Bob began watching TV before he had taken out the garbage.

To correct the misbehavior Mother should:

.... a. Take it out herself as its a small job.

.......✓....... b. Say to Bob, "What is the rule?"

Answer: b

Episode 2

Bob ignored Mother and continued watching TV.

To correct the misbehavior Mother should:

......✓...... a. Say, "Would you like to turn the TV off or should I?"

.... b. Take him by the ear and point him in the "right" direction.

Answer: a

Episode 3

Bob did not answer Mother, but continued watching the T.V. program.

To correct the misbehavior Mother should:

...✓...   a.   Turn off the TV.

....   b.   Say again, "Shall I turn it off or will you?"

Answer: a

Episode 4

After Mother turned off the TV, Bob turned to her and said, "If you weren't so lazy you would take the garbage out."

To correct the misbehavior Mother should:

....   a.   Say, "I do a lot more work than you. You're not a very appreciative young man."

...✓...   b.   Say unemotionally, "You could be right." Continue washing dishes.

Answer: b

Julie (fear of the dark)

Episode 1

Julie has been sleeping with Mother and Father because she is afraid of the dark. It seems that Mother and Father have no time alone.

To correct the misbehavior Mother should:

...✓...   a.   Say, "I know how you feel, but from now on you will have to sleep in your own bed. You can learn not to be afraid." Buy a night light for her room.

....   b.   Let her continue to sleep with her for when she gets older she will learn not to be afraid.

Answer: a

Episode 2

Julie sobbingly said, "I can't stay by myself. I'm afraid," even though the night light was on. She got in bed with Mother and Father.

To correct the misbehavior Mother should:

.... a. Cuddle her until she stops crying then ask her politely to return to her bed.

......✓...... b. Say, "You will learn." Immediately put her back in her own bed.

Answer: b

Episode 3

Julie followed Mother back and tried to get back in bed with her.

To correct the misbehavior Mother should:

......✓...... a. Immediately take Julie to her own room. Say nothing. Mother is to lock her own bedroom door on the way back.

.... b. Let her stay if she is this frightened.

Answer: a

Episode 4

When Julie found her way to her parents' bedroom barred by a locked door, she began to scream and pound on the door.

To correct the misbehavior Mother should:

......✓...... a. Turn the radio on to some soft music, put cotton in her ears, roll over and go to sleep.

.... b. Get Father to put her back in bed.

Answer: a

Jerry and Larry (fighting)

Episode 1

Larry pulled a face at Jerry. Jerry hit Larry. They both began yelling and hitting one another.

To correct the misbehavior Mother should:

.... a. Say, "Larry, stop pulling faces."

.... b. Say, "Boys, stop fighting in the house or take your fighting outside."

Answer: b

Episode 2

The boys got more noisy and fought harder. They stayed in the house.

To correct the misbehavior Mother should:

.... a. Take each by an arm firmly, but gently and put them outside.

.... b. Tell them once again to stop, for they apparently did not hear the first time.

Answer: a

Episode 3

Larry cried, "You don't love me Mother."

To correct the misbehavior Mother should:

.... a. Say nothing. Continue to put them outside.

.... b. Say, "Larry, you know Mother loves you very much."

Answer: a

Helen (sickness)

Episode 1

Helen who is seven got up this morning and cried, "My stomach hurts, I'm too sick to go to school."

To correct the misbehavior Mother should:

.... a. Say, "You must go to school today."

.... b. Say, "If you're sick you'll have to stay in bed."

Answer: b

Episode 2

At nine o'clock Helen suddenly became quite happy and said she wanted to watch TV.

To correct the misbehavior Mother should:

.... a. Say, "Sick children have to stay in bed so they will get well."

.... b. Let her watch TV.

Answer: a

Episode 3

When Mother refused to let her watch TV, she said, "You don't care about me. You just like to be mean."

To correct the misbehavior Mother should:

.... a. Say nothing. Think about the enjoyable time she had with her husband the last time they were out together.

.... b. Tell Helen she is an ungrateful, spoiled child.

Answer: a

Joan (temper tantrums)

Episode 1

Four-year-old Joan wanted to have Mother's purse. She picked it up and when Mother took it away from her she first yelled, "I want it," then screamed, threw herself on the floor and began kicking as she continued screaming.

To correct the misbehavior Mother should:

.... a. Give her the purse.
.... b. Walk into another room.

Answer: b

Episode 2

Joan followed Mother into the other room and started hitting her and yelling, "I hate you, I hate you."

To correct the misbehavior Mother should:

.... a. Slap her and tell her she is a naughty girl.
.... b. Say, "Would you like to go out by yourself or would you like me to put you out."

Answer: b

Episode 3

Joan did not leave the room. She continued to hit and yell at Mother.

To correct the misbehavior Mother should:

.... a. Take her by the shoulders and put her outside of the room, then lock the door, turn the radio up, and read a good book.
.... b. Start crying and say, "How can you hurt mommy like this?"

Answer: a

Jimmy (throwing food)

Episode 1

Three-year-old Jimmy heaped cereal on his spoon, then threw it the full length of the table.

To correct the misbehavior Mother should:

.... a. Say quietly, "Jimmy, would you like to stop throwing food or would you like to leave the table?"

        b. Say, "Good boys don't throw food."

Answer: a

Episode 2

Jimmy took his glass of milk and poured it on the floor.

    To correct the misbehavior Mother should:

        a. Take everything away from him and say, "That will teach you."

        b. Put him down from the table.

Answer: b

Episode 3

After Jimmy was put from the table, he went over to where Mother was sitting, started to cry and said, "I'll be good. I want to eat."

    To correct the misbehavior Mother should:

        a. Let him go to his own place at the table and continue eating.

        b. Say, "As long as you throw food you may not eat with the family. You can finish your dinner at the cupboard."

Answer: b

Andy (viciousness)

Episode 1

Mother asked Andy to settle down. He took a nut pick and while Mother was watching, gouged a big scratch in the walnut arm of her favorite chair.

    To correct the misbehavior Mother should:

        a. Say calmly, "Do you want to settle down or go to the time-out room?"

        b. Cry out, "How could you do that to my favorite chair?"

Answer: a

Episode 2

Andy immediately scratched the chair arm again.

To correct the misbehavior Mother should:

.... a. Take him by the hand, firmly but gently and put him in the time-out room.

.... b. Clobber him right good.

Answer: a

Episode 3

Andy immediately opened the door and came out.

To correct the misbehavior Mother should:

.... a. Push him back in and shut the door fast and hard. If his fingers get in the way — too bad.

.... b. Say calmly, "Would you like to stay in the room on your own or would you like Mother to lock the door?"

Answer: b

Episode 4

Andy did not go back in the time-out room. He stuck out his tongue at Mother.

To correct the misbehavior Mother should:

.... a. Take him by the shoulders, place him in the room and lock the door. Say calmly, "You may come out when you agree to settle down."

.... b. Start crying and say, "How can you be so mean?

Answer: a

What You Can Expect

As Mother starts responding differently to her misbehaving child, he will often get worse before he gets better. The reason for this is that the misbehaviors have rewarded the child so well in the past, i.e., in getting Mother to give undue service, that he thinks if he just tries harder she will respond in the old ways again.

The following is a hypothetical chart indicating the number of temper tantrums a child might exhibit when Mother first stops reinforcing them.

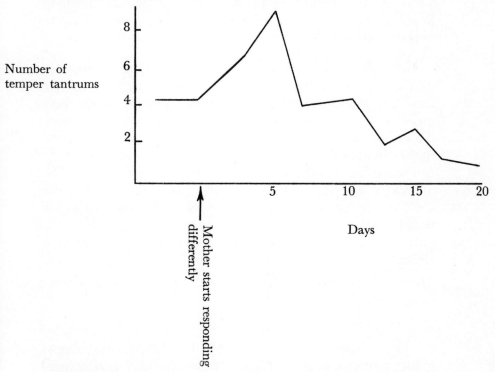

Mother may think she is doing something wrong when the child increases his misbehavior. Actually, this is good evidence that she is effectively disengaging from the child and he is striving extra hard to get her back into the old relationship. Mother needs to be extra firm with herself at this point and not allow the child to achieve his goal.

Some Cautions

It is suggested that Mother acquire the services of a good counselor or psychologist if the child is exhibiting extremely deviant behavior. Such a professional person can help Mother and the child directly or he may refer to another more qualified to work with the particular difficulty.

It is also recommended that Mother periodically take the child to a medical practitioner for a physical checkup. Most behavior problems of the child are due to problems in social interactions; however, occasionally they are due to organic difficulties.

Another caution: unless there is good, hard evidence Mother should not assume that the child's behavior problems are due to organic difficulties. Too often, mothers use this as an excuse, in their frustrations, to do nothing. This kind of an attitude tends to excuse the behavior of the highly manipulative child which gives him more power to tyrannize the family and to avoid his responsibilities. The author believes more damage is done by assuming that the child is organically inferior when he is not than by assuming that he is not when he is. The organically inferior child, the author is convinced, should be treated similarly to the normal child, except for differing levels and kinds of expectations.

Summary

This chapter has been written for the purpose of providing mothers with additional knowledge and some experience in applying the principles to some rather typical misbehavior cases of children. Chapter VII presents a summary of the basic principles in child rearing and Chapter VIII offers some additional helps in getting started in the endeavor of training and disciplining children, using the principles discussed in this book.

REFERENCES

Beier, Ernst G. *The Silent Language of Psychotherapy*. Chicago: Aldine Publishing Company, 1966.

Christensen, Oscar C. & Raymond Lowe. Information gained by the author from their lectures, discussions at family counseling centers and sessions at the Parent-Teacher Education Center, University of Oregon, Eugene, Oregon.

Dreikurs, Rudolph. *The Challenge of Parenthood*. New York: Duell, Sloan and Pearce, 1958.

Dreikurs, Rudolph. *Psychology in the Classroom, a Manual for Teachers*. New York: Harper and Row, Publishers, 1957.

Smith, Judith M. and Donald E. P. Smith. *Child Management, A Program for Parents*. Ann Arbor: Ann Arbor Publishers, 1967.

CHAPTER VII.

Some Do's and Don'ts — A Review

The following are some of the principles discussed in this book as they might be summarized through the eyes of your child.

Mother, Do:

1. Know that in order to better understand and help me you need to understand the A B C D goals of my misbehavior.

2. Know that I perceive myself, others and the world about me in my own special way, which may be logical or illogical. Help me to see logically.

3. Realize that I have a great amount of freedom to become what I want to become. My past history and biological characteristics provide possibilities and probabilities for me. They are not determiners of my behavior as some people would have you believe.

4. Realize that one of the best ways for me to correct my misbehaviors is for you to change the way you respond to them.

5. Understand how my order of birth in the family influences the way I perceive myself, my brothers and sisters, dad, you, and the world about me.

6. Treat me as an offspring of our Heavenly Father and as your brother/sister. Show me the respect that my brotherhood with you deserves. Respect my rights to grow and develop as you would like yours to be respected.

7. Realize that when I misbehave it is because I am discouraged about my place of belonging in the family and that misbehaviors are my clumsy, awkward ways of trying to make a place for myself.

8. Let me live in a home where there is order and routine. This will help me to be secure and live efficiently in an orderly society.

9. Watch your tone of voice. It tells me so much more about what you are feeling and thinking about me than the words you use.

10. Have the courage to tell me no when it is for my best good, even though I will sometimes really put the pressure on you. I want you to be concerned enough about my welfare that you will refuse my demands when it is best for me. Sometimes I will test you to see if you care enough to say no.

11. Listen to me. Talk *with* me rather than *to* me.

12. Train me in church and civic citizenship by allowing me to participate responsibly in our family home evenings and family councils.

13. Train me to relate to my fellow men in horizontal-cooperative ways rather than vertical-competitive ways by stressing cooperation, not competition, in the family.

14. Recognize me for my achievements rather than for my attempts to please you. If I learn to rely on pleasing you, I will try to please others rather than to do things for the sake of doing them well.

15. Know that if I am to feel secure I must also feel worthy.

16. Know that my measure of my own worth is gained through the eyes of those I love . If you value me and feel I am worthwhile, I will also tend to value and like myself.

17. Realize that if I don't feel worthy and accepted by those important in my life, my whole being will be consumed in striving to fulfill this need.

18. Realize that I learn best those things I want to learn.

19. Have faith and trust in me and I will have faith and trust in myself. This will give me the courage to meet your expectations and learn those things I must.

20. Arrange my toilet, closet hangers, eating utensils, and etc., so that I can do more things on my own rather than having to rely on older, bigger people which discourages self-reliance and lessens my feelings of self-worth.

21. Recognize the difference between my manipulating you for pampered service (setting a pattern of demanding you do for me those things I can do for myself) and the times when I do need help.

22. Give me help in such a way that I am stimulated toward greater independence and self-reliance rather than greater dependence.

23. Remember I am growing very fast. Keep pace with my abilities and my desire to do more things on my own.

24. Tell me when I have done something wrong as this helps me to develop a value system. Please do it with gentleness and understanding rather than with criticism and ridicule.

25. Correct me when we are in private for when I am corrected in front of others it hurts me. It makes me want to hurt you back.

26. Understand that sometimes I talk just to keep you busy with me, but at other times I sincerely have a difficult time expressing myself. Learn to know the difference.

27. Help me to see some of your faults and mistakes. This will give me the courage to keep trying when I make mistakes.

28. Apologize to me when you are in the wrong. I will feel warmer toward you and it will set a good example for me to follow.

29. Be firm with me. I need to know that you care enough about me to keep me within certain limits. It helps me to feel secure.

30. Wait until you are not angry with me before you try to train me. My own anger and yours will make it difficult for us to cooperate together. Do take the necessary action at the time, but let's discuss the situation later.

31. Know that my bad habits are like red flags signaling that there are problems which should be worked on. Improve our relationship first, then train me.

32. Help me to see that mistakes are common to all of us rather than emphasizing their sinful aspects. Help me to see that when I make mistakes it is not the end of the world. This will give me the courage to keep trying to improve to become, sometime in the eternities, perfect like our Heavenly Father.

33. Ignore my use of bad words at the time I speak them. Talk to me about them when we are friends together. If you laugh at me for using them, I will continue to use them to get your interest. If you get upset with me, they could become a tool I can use against you when I am angry with you.

34. Respond to my questions simply and directly. This will give me confidence in your desire to help me learn. Ignore my questioning, if it is for the purpose of keeping you busy with me.

35. Be consistent. Your behavior should be such that I can predict what you will do when I misbehave. I will feel you are concerned about me and that you hold to some basic values. This will help me to have faith in you and your guidance. It will also help to develop my own value system.

36. Expect me to experiment and make mistakes. Life is new to me. There is so much I am curious about and want to know. Encourage me to experiment by being lenient with my sometimes clumsy endeavors.

37. Let me experience the consequences of my own behavior whenever it is practical and possible. Sometimes I learn best by learning the hard way.

38. Remember that in most situations I know what is right from wrong. Much of what I do wrong is simply my attempts to keep you involved with me.

39. Remember, when we are arguing, that you are trying to win me to an agreement or understanding rather than attempting to defeat me.

40. Help me to see life realistically. Through assisting me to separate fact from opinion, I can better achieve this.

41. Realize that sometimes I can learn much better from my brothers and sisters than from you.

42. Act rather than talk-talk. I would rather you tell me once and then take firm, but gentle action than to nag me to death.

43. Respond with the unexpected when we are having difficulty. Usually the first impulse you act upon is the very thing I am trying to manipulate from you.

44. Treat all of us as a group when I am quarreling or fighting with my brothers and sisters. Often no one person is to blame, and if there is, you usually can't find out which one it is.

45. Have me pick up my own books, shoes, clothes, and etc. so that I will learn responsibility. If you do these things for me it teaches me to use you and others disrespectfully.

46. Have available for me to read only those things that will help me to build strong character. Be as careful with my reading material as you would with my sterilized eating utensils.

47. Put limits on my sensual desires for gratification rather than allowing me unlimited access to food, drink, and comfort. Such limits encourage me to greater self-discipline.

48. Give me a small allowance that is not subject to your bribery.

49. Let me earn additional money when it is needed. Don't give me all I want, for it will spoil me and teach me irresponsibility.

50. Stick with me if I ever get into real trouble. Let me know you are with me, but let me work myself out of the jam rather than you doing it for me.

51. Help me to experience the responsibility for my own actions when I try to get you to take my side against neighbors, teachers, or policemen.

52. Love me by respecting my own ability to grow, mature, and become self-reliant, rather than smothering me with a love which causes me to live as a dependent, emotional cripple.

53. When you set limits, provide me with choices (alternatives) so I will feel that I am in control of my own life. This will help me to learn to make decisions and we will avoid many conflicts.

54. Demand only occasionally when it is absolute necessary. When you make many demands, I feel frustrated, angry and as if I would like to defeat you.

55. Talk to me honestly, directly and simply. If you quibble with me or "beat around the bush," it encourages me to distrust you.

56. Acknowledge my positive contributions to the family. This will help me to feel responsible and worthwhile. I will tend to ally myself with the family.

57. Say, "I know it hurts, but you will soon get over it." It tells me you understand how I feel. It also gives me the courage to bear the pain, for I know it will leave.

58. Say, "I'll bet you can do it all by yourself." This tells me you have faith in me which helps me to have faith in myself. It encourages me to become more independent and self-reliant.

59. Teach me about Heavenly Father when I am young. If you wait until I am older, religion probably won't be a part of my value system. Other things will have become more important to me.

60. Allow me to live comfortably in the house. It shouldn't be so spotless that I am always afraid of incurring your anger when I relax.

Mother, Please:

1. Don't pamper me. Don't give me everything I want. Sometimes I am only testing you. If you do give in to me it will encourage me to believe the world owes me a living and this will lead me to an unhappy adult life full of conflict with my fellow men.

2. Don't nag me. When you nag at me, I will usually try to keep you involved by appearing deaf.

3. Don't be too concerned about the amount of time we have together. The main thing, after all, is what we do when we are together.

4. Don't use force with me or retaliate against me. I will learn much faster and be much more willing to do what you want when you lead me.

5. Don't get too "shook up" when I tell you "I hate you." I don't really mean this. What I do mean is that I feel hurt and I want to hurt you back. If you show hurt, this stimulates me to keep trying to hurt you.

6. Don't give me undue service when I am sick. This stimulates me to become sickly in order to manipulate special service and attention from you.

7. Don't do those things for me that I can do for myself. When you do for me what I can do for myself, it makes me feel smaller than I really am and lowers my self-esteem.

8. Don't punish me. When you punish me it tells me that I have the right to punish other people, including my younger brothers and sisters. It also encourages me to dislike you as I tend to equate you with punishment. There are better ways of keeping me within the limits you set.

9. Don't reward me with symbols such as money when you try to get me to do what you want. This confuses my value system and can make it very difficult for me, when I grow up, to put the important things first in my life.

10. Don't get angry with me. When you are angry, I can usually defeat you. It teaches me that being powerful is important.

11. Don't spank me. When you spank me, it trains me to be afraid of those bigger than I and I become either shy and backward or aggressive and brutal. Spanking tends to make me angry towards people.

12. Don't quarrel in front of me with daddy because this tends to get me involved too, which usually complicates the situation rather than making it better.

13. Don't help me with my homework. I can use it as a tool to defeat you or get you to give me service. Also, trying to please you becomes so important it becomes difficult for me to do my lessons well. It is also hard for you to have patience with me at the end of a long day. The homework should be between my teacher and me. Probably the best thing you can do is to help me set up a schedule for studying and then see that I stick to it.

14. Don't give me the impression that you are superior to me. This encourages me to believe in a world of superiors and inferiors and causes me to be insecure. It also makes it hard for me to relate to my fellow men as truly brothers and sisters.

15. Don't compare me with anyone, especially my brothers and sisters. Comparing discourages me partly because it indicates that you relate to others in a vertical fashion; therefore, I am never sure of my place with you.

16. Don't tax my honesty too much, especially when I am little. Sometimes I don't know what is really so, and your demands will sometimes frighten me into telling lies.

17. Don't make promises without keeping them.

18. Don't pity me. This makes me feel smaller than I really am. It discourages me and helps me to think little of myself.

19. Don't let my fears control you. When I am little I will sometimes truly be afraid. If you are calm and serene, my fears will leave. But if you get concerned or give me special privileges, my fears will stay with me because with them I can manipulate special involvement or favors from you.

20. Don't excuse my present irresponsible behavior by emphasizing my difficulties in the past. I am creative and have much freedom to become the kind of person I and you want me to be. I can rise above poor past experiences.

REFERENCES

Ansbacher, Heinz L. and Rowena R. Ansbacher. *The Individual Psychology of Alfred Adler*. New York: Basic Books, Inc., Publishers. 1956.

"A Memorandum From Your Child," Adapted From *The King's Business*. The Bible Institute of California, Publishers. (A Class Handout at the Parent-Teacher Education Center, University of Oregon, Eugene, Oregon.)

Critique on the Application of Hypotheses and Theory on Dynamics. From *Summaries of Scientific Papers*, A.P.A. 8, 1957, pp. 97-98.

Dreikurs, Rudolph. *The Challenge of Parenthood*. New York: Duell, Sloan and Pearce. 1958.

"How To Ruin Your Children," A Pamphlet distributed by the Houston, Texas Police Department under the title, "Twelve Rules for Raising Delinquent Children." Original Sources unknown.

Fisher, Siegfried. "Ten Axioms in Human Behavior," A Paper presented at the American Psychiatric Association Annual Meeting, May 13-17, 1957.

Seymour, F.J.C. "Ten Commandments For Resolving Conflict Situations," An Address given at the National Educational Association Center in Washington D.C., November 11-14, 1957.

CHAPTER VIII.

Getting Started

Introduction

It is difficult for anyone to change his behavior. Everyone is bound by habits and when attempts are made to change them, effort, energy, time, and sometimes pain are required. This you will find as you work at changing the way you respond to your misbehaving child (ren); however, the discovery of more harmonious relationships will make the endeavor well worth while. The purpose of this chapter is to help Mother sharpen her perceptions so that she can see more clearly her relationships with her misbehaving child(ren) and arrange her environment so that she will be encouraged to work differently with him. The purpose then is to help Mother respond differently to her children when they are misbehaving. These helps are presented in six steps.

Step 1 — A Self-Examination

The following are statements with which some people usually tend to agree while others usually tend to disagree. It is a knowledge and attitude check of your understanding of the position taken in this book. Indicate with an X your approximate degree of agreement or disagreement.

A Knowledge and Attitude Check

	Agree			Disagree		
1. Do not do for the child what he can do for himself.	3	2	1	1	2	3
2. The first thing you think of to do with the child who is misbehaving usually reinforces the misbehavior.	3	2	1	1	2	3

3. Mother is usually equally as responsible as the child for his misbehaviors.
   3   2   1   1   2   3

4. Most mothers talk too much.
   3   2   1   1   2   3

5. Mother should not help the child with his homework even when it is requested.
   3   2   1   1   2   3

6. There is always a better way of disciplining a child than by spanking.
   3   2   1   1   2   3

7. Mother should not compare the child with anyone else.
   3   2   1   1   2   3

8. As a mother, your first responsibility is to the whole family, not to the individual child.
   3   2   1   1   2   3

9. There are usually better ways to motivate a child to learn than through the use of rewards.
   3   2   1   1   2   3

10. A child only learns well what he wants to learn.
   3   2   1   1   2   3

11. Humiliation and ridicule are inefficient ways to discipline a child.
   3   2   1   1   2   3

12. Most children know what is right and wrong.
   3   2   1   1   2   3

13. Repeating a command is one of the best ways to get a child to disobey it.
   3   2   1   1   2   3

14. The surest way to get
your child to change his   3   2   1   1   2   3
behavior is for you to
change your behavior as
you respond to his dis-
turbing behavior.

15. The child who misbe-
haves is discouraged   3   2   1   1   2   3
about his place of be-
longing in the family.

The more you have checked three under agree, the more you understand and are in agreement with the principles suggested in this book and are ready to go on to Step 2.

Step 2 — Observation of Others

This step is to help you sharpen your perceptions of the patterns of interaction between other mothers and their children. It is suggested that you observe for one week other mothers as they interact with their children in the neighborhood, supermarket, church, etc. The following are ten questions you might ask yourself as you observe:

1. What is the general attitude of the mothers toward their children? Are they impatient, nagging, cross, or anxious? Or are they friendly, cooperative, courteous and pleasant? Do the mothers express love and a liking for their children?

2. How many try to demand or force their children to respect them? How many, rather than trying to demand respect of their children, attempt to earn it?

3. How many mothers attempt to control every little movement of their children? How many of them are continually ordering their children rather than making requests of them?

4. How many give in to their first impulse when responding to their misbehaving children? How many feed into every whim or appetite? How many are tyrannized by their children?

5. How many mothers attempt to get their children to obey them through the use of bribes or rewards? For example, how many mothers say, "If you will be good, I will buy you a candy bar?" Watch how the children react to the bribes. Do they learn to be bad for the sake of getting more rewards?

6. How many appear to feel that the only way they can change the misbehavior of their children is through physical punishment? How many feel that a good whipping is what children need when they misbehave? When this does occur, notice how the parents feel after they have spanked their children in contrast to how the children feel.

7. When mothers are disciplining their children, how many seem to be reacting to what they think others expect of them rather than what is best for their children?

8. How many belittle their children in front of others? How many correct their children in curt tones? How many mothers ridicule their children into submission in front of others?

9. How many mothers are over demanding of the child and expect perfection beyond his age capability?

10. How many compare one child with another as they attempt to enforce good behavior?

If you are careful in your observations, you will see interactions between mothers and their children more completely and understandably. The next step is a little harder.

Step 3 — Observation of Self

For the next two days it is suggested that you use the above questions in looking at your interactions with your own children. This will be harder than step two, for you are much more emotionally involved with your own children than you are with your neighbor's or those whom you do not know. Many times, because of our emotional involvement and past habitual ways of responding to our children, our perceptions become dulled. This step will take effort and courage in order for you to see the total picture of what is going on. However, you will be well rewarded.

Step 4 — Write Out Observations

Mother, after you have spent two days observing yourself and your children using the ten questions, the next logical step is for you to write down your observations in very specific and concrete terms. The advantage of written notes is that it disciplines you to more accurate observation and, as you write, ideas will tend to come to you suggesting plans for changing your behavior and, therefore, your children's misbehavior.

As you record your observations remember that the child's basic striving is to find a secure place in the family, especially a place with you. Remember also that his behaviors are purposeful and express his attitudes, expectations and goals in the family. Therefore, behavior has meaning. It is not determined by past experience, nor is it random. Your misbehaving child is a creative child with a relatively large amount of freedom to decide what his actions are to be. He is not a mechanical robot directed by others or controlled by his past experiences. The child is active in the environment and just as he is in part molded by mother's behavior he is, to a large extent, often molding or manipulating Mother.

When recording, place the emphasis on the child's interaction with Mother or with other children and include their responses to him.

Guides to Sound Observation

Your observations will tend to be of more value to you if you do the following:

1. See the situation through the eyes of the child as well as through your own.

2. Look for the child's purposes, the A B C D goals of his misbehavior.

3. Observe all the important actions. Include the typical and usual behavior as well as the unusual, for every expressed mood of the child has meaning.

4. Realize that the child's behavior is creative as he attempts to find his place in the family. His responses are not robot-like or random.

5. Be careful to look for patterns of behavior. Patterns have reference to actions that tend to occur over and over.

6. Be somewhat aware of the child's level of mental and physical development.

The following are some characteristics of a good write-up and are intended to guide you as you record the significant interactions between you and your misbehaving child-(ren).

Guidelines to a Good Write-Up

1. A good write-up will include the setting for the action, the time of day, the place, and possibly the date.

2. Both the actions of the child are described and the reactions of others as they respond to him. At this point in the write-up, interpretations or guesses as to what things are going on are to be only tentatively made. Such general words as angry, embarrassed, shy, etc. should not be included.

3. Key words of the child and Mother and/or others involved in the interaction are included exactly as they are stated.

4. All communicative cues are included: tone of voice, gestures, facial expressions, and postures that indicate feelings.

5. The write-up covers all meaningful action so that in effect a short story is told.

6. After the story is told as objectively as possible, interpretations may be made. It should be remembered, however, that these interpretations are only guesses as to what is going on in the interaction. The observer should be continually open to new evidence. The interpretations should be made within the framework of the philosophy suggested in this book. Emphasis should be on looking for the A B C D goals of the misbehaving child and his feelings concerning his place in the family. Mother or other people feeding into the goals of the child should of course be noted as evidence.

7. After patterns emerge, a plan of action for correcting the misbehavior of the child can be made. The emphasis is on Mother changing her behavior so she is not feeding into and reinforcing the misbehaviors of the child. The child is also encouraged to more constructive ways of responding.

The following is a format that Mother might use as she records her observations. Immediately following the format are two examples of how it could be used.

A PLAN FOR ACTION

	OBSERVATION	GUESS	WHAT TO DO	
Incident (Time & Place)	Specific Behavior	Goals of the Misbehavior	To Discourage Poor Behavior	To Encourage Better Behavior
1.	Child's Actions: Mother's Reactions: a. Feelings b. Behavior			

A PLAN FOR ACTION

	OBSERVATION	GUESS	WHAT TO DO	
Incident (Time & Place)	Specific Behavior	Goals of the Misbehavior	To Discourage Poor Behavior	To Encourage Better Behavior
1. 10:00 a.m. - 11:00 a.m. our house	Child's Actions: *While I was making cookies Jerry kept knocking on the door. When I went to the door he would run away giggling. He did this off and on for one hour.* Mother's Reactions: a. Feelings: *Annoyed, irritated, "That darn kid."* b. Behavior: *Went to the door and said, "You stop that Jerry I am too busy for any of this foolishness."*	*Goal A* *Jerry is keeping me busy with him.*	*Keep working at my cookies. No matter how hard it is I will say nothing and not go to the door. I won't even look up.*	*Talk with Jerry for awhile at bedtime concerning those things that interest him.*

A PLAN FOR ACTION

	OBSERVATION	GUESS	WHAT TO DO	
Incident (Time & Place)	Specific Behavior	Goals of the Misbehavior	To Discourage Poor Behavior	To Encourage Better Behavior
1. 3:00 *p.m.*	Child's Actions: *Five-year old Jannette came to me with tears in her eyes saying, "John hit me hard."* Mother's Reactions: a. Feelings: *Poor Jannette. That mean kid John.* b. Behavior: *"You tell John to come here right this minute."*	*Goal A* *Jannette's getting me to give her undue service.*	*Say, "You're big enough to work it out with John."*	*Tonight sit between John and Jannette and tell the two of them some stories.*

Step 5 — Associate with Other Parents

This step is crucial. It is most helpful for Mother to associate with other parents who are interested in improving their relationships with their disturbing children. Through encouraging one another, by giving emotional and moral support, each has more strength to go about the very difficult task of changing behavior. They can also help one another achieve greater insight.

Mother can associate herself with other mothers in the neighborhood, with certain organizations in the church that have an interest in parents and children, or with PTA Groups. The following are guidelines which will increase the probability of your study group becoming successful.

Guidelines for a Mothers' Study Group

1. Each mother should have the book *Mission for Mother*. This will encourage study and a commitment to the group since each will have made an investment in it.

2. The organization should be informal; however, the group may wish to select a discussion leader and possibly a recorder to write down the understandings achieved and recommendations made. This will give continuity and stimulate progress.

3. Each member should understand that this approach is just applying good, common sense in child rearing.

4. Use only the approach suggested in this book. If the group discusses other approaches, it will tend to get "bogged down" in conflict and little will be accomplished. Encourage the idea that the group is not after consensus of agreement. The purpose is to work toward a better understanding and better relationships with misbehaving children. The members can, of course, choose any procedure they wish in dealing with their children, although the pur-

pose of this study group is to gain a better understanding using the approach discussed in this book.

5. The group should use the experiences of group members. These experiences may be offered slowly at first until the group members become familiar and feel safe with one another.

6. There is to be no attempt to find fault or to blame. The emphasis in the group should be on (a) what is going on? and (b) what can Mother do to change the situation?

7. Remember brothers and sisters in the family situation being discussed. They can have as much impact as Mother on the misbehaving child.

8. Simple and fascinating concepts with which mothers in the study group can start their discussions, concepts which they can feel are well within their understanding, are those of family constellation (order of birth) and the A B C D goals of misbehaving children.

9. Do not try to cover everything in one session. The focus of the group should be on one principle or, when working with a mother and her misbehaving child, on one particular misbehavior. For example, if Mother is having trouble with Johnny eating, going to bed, sassing and fighting, the study group should help Mother with only one thing at a session, i.e., Johnny's poor eating habits. This way the situation becomes manageable and it gives Mother confidence that it can be handled, whereas if she tried to change her behavior on all points at once she would tend to become discouraged and possibly give up.

10. The general atmosphere of the study group should be that of cooperation and respect . It should be devoid of blame, vertical relationships, and competition. If there is cooperation and respect, the study group will be very productive.

Step 6 — Visit Family Education Centers

Another step that some mothers may be able to take is that of participating in an open forum type family education center using principles discussed in this book. In such a center, Mother can check out her understandings, learn more, observe theory put into practice and cooperate with other interested parents in working with her own or another family "in focus." The family in focus is the family being counseled. Through active participation with others and seeing changes take place in other families, Mother is stimulated to work at making changes in her own family. She also finds that she is not alone, as other mothers have the same problems. This gives her added courage to work at changing the misbehavior of her children.

There are only a few open forum type family education centers in the United States. One of these, sponsored by the department of Child Development and Family Relationships, is located on the Brigham Young University campus in Provo, Utah. Contact your local school district or community mental health center to determine whether or not this service is offered in your area.

Guides to Encouraging the Child

As you begin to work at changing the behavior of your child, it is important that you remember that his level of courage must be fairly high to facilitate his risking change. Just as it will take courage for you to change your behavior with him, it will require courage of him. The following are guidelines to assist you in stimulating courage in your child.

1. The child must have many more experiences with success than failure if he is to have courage to attack problems of life with zest. Mother should train the child so that the tasks required of him are sequentially and psychologically paced to allow a much higher number of success than failure exper-

iences. It is suggested by some that the average child must have about three success experiences to one failure if he is to have the courage to keep striving and developing at a high rate.

2. Mother must value the child as he is with all of his faults, errors, and inadequacies. If Mother values the child, the child will value himself and this will give him courage to keep trying.

3. Mother must have faith in the child and his ability. This gives him the courage to have faith in himself. The child will tend to mirror Mother's faith in him. This becomes his adopted faith in himself.

4. Give recognition for effort as well as for a job well done. Sometimes the child learns much more from attempting something, even though he does not do it well, than from the actual completion of the task.

5. Mother can utilize the whole family unit to provide opportunitites for the child to grow and develop. If the child can contribute in a responsible way to the well-being of the family and the responses of the other members indicate and recognize this contribution, the child's courage will be enhanced. This sets a pattern for the child's attitude towards himself and life beyond the family.

6. Emphasize cooperation in the family. The family unit should be well integrated — an equal place for all — so that the child can be sure of belonging. The home atmosphere should be free of competition. This will give the child courage to try without fear of failure because he knows that he can fail and still be accepted.

7. The child will be encouraged to grow and develop if Mother emphasizes the child's assets and strengths rather than his bad habits and weaknesses.

8. The child will be encouraged if he knows that Mother understands him, that she can see through his eyes. Also, he will be encouraged when Mother uses his interests rather than her own for stimulating his growth.

Summary

This chapter has indicated to Mother some steps she can take to get started in changing her behavior and, therefore, the misbehaviors of her children. It is important that she sharpen her perception as to what is going on between herself and her children when they misbehave. It is also important that she develop skills in understanding her children's world, including the goals of their misbehavior. One thing that will greatly facilitate for Mother the improvement of her ability to put the ideas discussed in this book into effect, is that of banding together with other mothers interested in improving the training and disciplining of their children. Mothers together can support and encourage one another.

Mother, you have one of the most stimulating, responsible and worthwhile professions ever entrusted to mankind, for you are attempting to rear children so that they will eventually be prepared to enter again into the kingdom of our Heavenly Father. Yours is not an easy task. It requires clear perception, firmness, respect for yourself and your children, and *persistence*. Because your children are spiritual offspring of our Heavenly Father and blessed with free agency, your relationships with them will be constantly fluid. They will involve recurring tests for you, for your children are highly creative. If you keep working with them and preserve your faith in them as they grow to adulthood, their beauty and your relationships with them will bring much happiness. It is hoped that the principles discussed in this book will help you to achieve such joy.

REFERENCES

Bullard, Maurice L. "Suggestions to Leaders Starting Parent-Child Study Groups," A Pamphlet prepared for use of parents' study groups in Corvallis, Oregon.

Dinkmeyer, Don and Rudolph Driekurs. *Encouraging Children to Learn: The Encouragement Process.* Englewood Cliffs: Prentice-Hall, Inc., 1963.

Grey, Loren., "What Do You Think?" A Parents Self Rating Sheet. Prepared in San Fernando Valley State College, Los Angeles, California and used at the Parent-Teacher Education Center, University of Oregon, Eugene, Oregon, by parents and teachers.

"Some Homework for Parents," A Pamphlet distributed in the Parent-Teacher Education Center, University of Oregon, Eugene, Oregon, based on F. H. Richardson, *How to Get Along With Children.* Atlanta; Tupper and Love, 1954.

Index

-A-

Activities, 16
Accidents during training, 81
Action, figures, 256, 257, 258
Adam, 34
Adler, Dr. Alfred, vii
Adlerian Family Counseling, 73
Adolescent, 55
Adulthood, freedom of, 64
Aesthetic, stimulate an appreciation for
    things, 102
Affection, 5
    training to give and accept, 99
Allen, Richard, viii
American society, tragedies in, 50
Anarchy, 51
Andy (viciousness), episodes of, 235
Ansbacher, Heinz L., 31, 248
Ansbacher, Rowena R., 31, 248
Anxiety, 4, 9
Atmosphere, 262
Attention, 58

-B-

Baby, another arrival of a new, 105
Baby talk, 85
    how to treat, 186
Bad habit, play down, 53
Balana, principle of, 15
Bandura, Albert, 114
Barbara, the case of, 224
Bashfulness, 181
Basic assumptions of misbehavior, 116,
    117
Beautiful, perception of the, 102
Beauty, 102
Bedtime, 105
Bedwetting, how to treat, 133-135
Behavior, change in, 8
    defiant, 237
    has meaning, 253
    is purposeful, 18
    patterns of, 254
    perfectionistic, 171
    positive, 54
    set boundaries for, 63
Behavior
    task of changing, 259
    unconstructive, 59
Behaviorists, 19
Beier, Ernst G., 31, 73, 239
Beliefs, religious, 32
Benevolence, 5
Bennion, Adam S., 17
Berrett, William E., 17
Beyer, Evelyn, 114

Bill, the case of, 212
Biological characteristics, 19
Birth, order of, 24
Bob (disobeys), episodes of, 229
Bobby, the case of, 221
Body, physical, 33
Book of Mormon, The, 17, 39
Bossing, 122
Brigham Young University, 261
Brutality, 138-140
Bullard, Maurice L., 264
Burton, Alma P., 44

-C-

Challenge of Parenthood, The, 31, 114,
    239, 248
Character, traits of, 5
Charity, 7
Celestial kingdom, 45
Cheek, turning the other, 4
Children, 14
Child, a brutal, 139
Child, dependent, 144
Child, guides to encouraging the, 261
    "Life Style" of the, 22
    pampered, 57, 89
    respect the, 49
    rearing, some practical first principles
        in successful, 52ff
    the rebellious, 123
    the shy, 181
    bribing, 69
    Management, 239
Choice, 19, 61
    provide the child with, 45
Chores, household, guidelines for, 88
Christ, 6, 34, 42, 43
Christ's Ideals for Living, by Obert C.
    Tanner, 17
Christensen, Dr. Alfred, vii
Christensen, Oscar C., 73, 239
Christian, 4
Citizenship, Church, 46
Commandment, the great, 36
Communication, total, 56
Community, Parent-Teacher Education
    Center, vii
Compassion, 7
Competition, 23, 30, 49, 262
Conduct, proper sexual, 177
Consequences, logical, 60
    guidelines to, 61
    natural, 59, 60
Consistency, 57
Consistent, be, 56
Constellation, the family, 24, 28

Cooperation, 23, 193
  in the family, 262
  revolt against, 148
  train for, not competition, 49
Conversation, lively, 101
Counseling, group, 8
Counselor, 91
Counterhurt, 123
Courageousness, stimulate, in the child, 47
Cowdery, Oliver, 41
Creativity, 19
  encourage, 101
Criminal, 190
Cripples, emotional, 13
Criticism, eliminate, 53
Crying, how to treat, 204, 205
Cues, communicative, 255
Curiosity, encourage, 101
  sexual, 177

-D-

Dan, the case of, 211
Darrell, the case of, 219
Decision-making, 70
Deformities, biological, 29
Dependence, how to treat, 143, 144
Dependency, 50, 139
Deprivation, 12
Destiny, 38
Diane, the case of, 215
Dinkmeyer, Dan, 31, 114, 264
Disagreement, 66
Discouragement, 48, 124
Discouragement Process, The, 31
Discoveries of the Prophet Joseph Smith, 44
Disobedience, 149
Disobedient child, how to treat the, 147-149
Dominance, over a child, 162
Dominate, do not, 65
Dominion, unrighteous, 38
Do's and Don'ts, a review, 240ff
Dreikurs, Dr. Rudolph, vii, 31, 73, 114, 240, 248, 264
Dressing, children, 90
Driving force, the basic, 18

-E-

Eating, children's, 91
Eating habits, guidelines for proper, 92, 93
Ecstacy, 14
Educating Children in Nursery Schools and Kindergartens, 114
Education for Freedom, by Ludia Sicher, 17
Educational Psychology, 114
Emotion, negative, 52
Encouraging Children to Learn, 114
Enemies, love your, 6
Estate, second, 42

Evil, 9
Existence, purposes of, 33
Experiences, have positive, 127
  housekeeping, 110

-F-

Failure, 26
Faith, 21, 261
Faith, three steps to encourage, 100
Faithfulness, 7
Family, 49
Family Council, 70, 83
  guidelines for a, 71, 72
    Family Education Centers, visit, 261
Family Institution, 28
Family unit, 261
  an eternal institution, 42
Fear, 9
  and anxiety, how to treat, 150, 151
  don't be panicked by, 55
Fearful, 55
  procedure to use when a child is, 151
Feelings, concomittant, 47
Fellowmen, we should judge our, 9
Female, mission of the, 97
Fiction, 162
Fighting, 66
Fingernails, biting, how to treat, 136
First born, the characteristics of, 25
Fisher, Siegfried, 247
Flattery, of others, 13
Foundation, a psychological, 18 ff
Foundation, the religious, 32 ff
Franke, Viktor E., 20, 31
Free agency, 50, 53
  of the child,
  the fundamental principle, 35 ff
Free will, 19
Freedom, 36
  misuse of, 60
Freudians, 19
Friendliness, 5
Frustration, 12

-G-

Getting up, in the morning, 94
Glasser, William, 31
Goal A, attention, 119
Goal B, to boss mother, 122
Goal C, to counterhurt, 123
Goal D, to appear disabled, 124
Goals, child's, 18
  figure, 120
God, 34
  existence of, 33
  love for, 112
  reverence for, 1
  stimulate a belief and a faith in, 100
Godhood, major purpose of, 36
  rights of, 35
"Good" child, the, how to treat, 152, 153
Good Life, The, by E. Jordan, 17

Goodness, 153
Gospel, doctrines of the, 100
Gospel Ideals, 44
Gore, Lillian L., 114
Grey, Loren, 263
Group, treat all as, when they fight, 66
Grow, courage to continually strive to, 112
Guide, figure, 126
Guidelines, to a good write-up, 253
Guilt, artificial, 4

-H-

Habits, predictable, 51
Hall, Calvin S., 31
Handicap, physical or mental, 54
Handicapped child, the, 108
Happiness, 9
    cannot be without free agency, 38
Harry, the case of, 225
Heavenly Father, 10, 43
Helen (sickness), episodes, 233
Henley, William Ernest, 21, 31
History, past, 19
Hitler, 10
Holy Spirit of Promise, 42
Honesty, 8, 112
Homework, 111
Hostility, overt, 53
Humility, 1

-I-

Imagination, 162
Imitation, 75
Improvement Era, 11
Inabilities, 144
Inadequacy, feeling of, 155
Incompetency, 29
Inconsistency, 57
Identity, establishing, 78
Individual, democratic, 5
Individual Psychology of Alfred Adler, The, 31
Ineptitude, how to treat, 154-156
Independence, stimulate, 89
    in the child, 46
Inferiority, feelings of, 29
Initiative, encourage, 101
Insecurity, feelings of, 29
Integrity, 8
Interaction, 137
Invictus, poem, 20
Involvement, emotional, 253
    watch your, 58
Irregularities in speech, 185
Irresponsibility, 50
Israel, mothers of, 12
Items, how to treat the leaving of, 159, 160

-J-

Jane and Bob, the case of, 210
Jane, the case of, 208, 213

Jean, the case of, 223
Jerry and Larry (fighting), episodes of, 232
Jerry, the case of, 218
Jesus, 2, 3
Jim, the case of, 206
Jimmy (throwing food), episodes of, 234
Joan (temper tantrums), episodes of, 233
Joan, the case of, 217
John the Beloved, 10
Johnny, the case of, 207
Jordan, E., 17
Joy, 34
Juliet (fear of the dark), episodes of, 230

-K-

Kingdom of heaven, 41
Kinship, feeling, with others, 5
Knowledge and attitude, a, 249
Koury, Rose, 114
Krawiec, 31

-L-

Language development, 84
Learning, principles of, 74 ff
    traits that encourage, 77
    traits that tend to discourage, 76
Life, balance of, 16
Lights, 106
Limitations, of behavior of child, 63
Lindzy, Gardner, 31
Love, 8
    for God, 1
Lowe, Dr. Raymond, vii, 73, 239
Lydia, the case of, 216
Lying, how to treat, 161

-M-

Maladjustment, among children, 28
Man, characteristics of, 32
    spiritual child of God, 32
    who is, 32
Mankind, compassion for, 4, 112
Mark, the case of, 227
Martyr complex, 22
Mary, the case of, 226
Man's Search for Meaning, 20, 31
Maslow, A. H., 17
Masturbation, how to treat, 163, 164
Maturation, 76
McDonald, Fredrick J., 114
McKay, David O., xi, 35, 38
Mead, Dr. Eugene, viii
Mealtime, 91
Middle child, the characteristics of, 25
Melchizedek Priesthood Lessons, The, 115
Misbehaving, how Mother should respond differently to, 249 ff
Misbehavior, 18, 28, 117, 146
    ABCD goals of, 30
    basic guidelines for not reinforcing, 58
    consequences of, 60
    correcting the, 116 ff

Misbehavior, revengeful pattern of, 123
    the basic approach to, 58
    what should Mother do?, 125
Mistakes, minimize, 54
Montagu, N. F. Ashley, 114
Moroni, 39
Morrill, Reed, viii
Mother, 5, 45, 46, 47, 49, 52, 54, 57, 58,
    59
    as a teacher, 76
    child's relationship with, 50
    how to treat when children correct,
        141, 142
    inconsistent, 56
    perfectionistic, 48
Motherhood, challenge of, 43
    effective, vii
    greatest of all vocations, xi
Motivation and Personality, by A. H.
    Maslow, 17
Motor control, training for, 79

-N-
Narrowness, 14
Nature, an eternal, 14
Needs, two basic, 18
Neglect, 139
Nephites, 39
No, be courageous enough to say, 57
Nursery School Settings, 114
Nursing, of a child, 102 ff
    schedule, advantages of, 103

-O-
Objectives, of Mother, 1 ff
    principles of attaining, 45 ff
Observation, of self, 252
Observations, guides to sound, 254
    write out, 253
One Thousand Quotable Poems, 31
Oneness, feeling of, 6
Only child, the characteristics of, 27
Openness, 14, 113
Order, train the child to respect, 51
Overconcern, parental, 164
Overpermissive parent, 132

-P-
Pampering, 25
Parenthood, eternal, 42
    responsibility of, 42, 49
Parents, associate with other, 259
Passivity, 53
Past oriented, 173
Patience, 5
Patterns, 255
Paul, 7, 8, 32
People, indecisive, 46
Perceptions, biased, 22
Perfectionist, how to treat the, 170, 171
Persistence, 127, 263
Person, worth as a, 78
Peter, 2, 10

Pettiness, 14
Petting, 164
Pharisees, 3
Piano practicing, 106
Pity, has many pitfalls, 54
"Pitytrap," 54
Play, children's, 80
Playmates, 86
Potential godhood, 35
Polaroid camera, 78
Practicing, time for, 107
Pressure, from the child, 54
Priesthood and You, The, 11
Principles, applying the, 74 ff
Principles, for child rearing, 45 ff
Principles, guiding, 22
"Problem-centered," 13
Problems, efficiency in solving, 13, 113
    religious, 36
Procreation, in the resurrected state, 42
Progress, courage to continually, 10
Property, how to treat destruction of, 145
Psychological clinics, 46
Psychologists, 9, 57, 78
Psychology in the Classroom, 31, 239
Psychology, Systems and Theories of, 31
Psuedo deaf mute, how to treat, 185
PTA, 258
Punishment, should be avoided, 67
Purposes, man's, 33
-Q-
Quarreling, how to treat, 165-167
Quarrels, advantages of staying out of
    children's, 166
    Mother's involvement in, 66
    problems when Mother gets involved
    in, 166
-R-
React, three general ways to, 18
Reality, 19, 112
Reality Therapy, 31
Relationship, train the child when the, is
    good, 52 ff
    vertical, 49
Relationships, interpersonal, 5, 9
    social, 153
Repentance, need for, 11
Requests, make them reasonable and
    sparse, 53
Responsibility, of everyone, how to treat,
    172, 173
    man's, to himself, 39
Restitution, 191
Revenge, 190
Revengeful, 146
Rewards, problems in using, 68
Rewarding, use care in, 68
Rights of others, train the child to respect
    the, 50
Rod, the case of, 214
Routine, 51
Rule oriented, 173

-S-

Sacrament meeting misbehavior, how to treat, 174, 175
Salvation, 33, 41
Sarcasm, 101
Satan, 2, 37
Schedule, should be established in the home, 51
School, how to prepare the child for, 108 ff
Scribes, 3
Self-abasement, 1
Self-discipline, guiding the child to, 96
Self-reliance, 12, 113
Self, respect and acceptance of, 1, 112
Self-worth, 47
Selfishness, 14
Servant, unprofitable, 41
Services, counseling, 46
Seymour, F. J. C., 248
Sex differences, 24
Sex education, 96 ff
Sex, guidelines for teachers, 98, 99
Sexual misbehavior, how to treat, 176
Shame, crippling, 4
Sharing, guidelines for, 87, 88
Sheryl, the case of, 220
Shoes, 159
Showing off, how to treat, 178, 179
Shyness, how to treat, 180, 181
Sicher, Lydia, 17
Sickness, how to treat, 182, 183
Silent Language of Psychotherapy, The, 31, 73, 239
Sloppiness, 144
Smith, Donald E. P., 238
Smith, Eldred G., 11
Smith, Joseph, 10, 34
Smith, Judith M., 239
Social Learning and Personality Developments, 114
Social pressures, 57
Social skills, 83
"Sociality," of the Gods, 35
Socially rooted, the child is, 21
Society, 23
Speech problem, how to treat, 184-186
Spontaneity, 15
Stalling, how to treat, 187, 188
Standards, 11
    do not set too high or too low, 48
    for living together, 82
    setting of, 127
Stealing, how to treat, 189-191
Stubbornness, how to treat, 192
Study Group, guidelines for a Mothers', 259
Stupidity, how to treat, 194, 195
Stuttering, how to treat, 185
Subtlety, 26
Success, 23

Sue ("Bugging Mommy"), episodes of, 228
Superiority, moral, 22
Swine, herd of, 34
Sympathy, 55

-T-

Talents, development of child's, 106
    parable of the, 39, 40
Talking, quit and act, 62
Tanner, Obert C., 17
Tantrums, temper, 64
Teachings of the Book of Mormon, by William E. Berrett, 17
Teenagers, 57
Temper, a quick, 77
    tantrums, 86
    tantrums, chart of, 237
    tantrums, how to treat, 198, 199
Temple, Christ drives money-changers from the, 3
Ten Commandments, 36
Terry, the case of, 222
The Holy Bible, 17
Theories of Personality, 31
Thumb-sucking, how to treat, 196, 197
Tidiness, 95
Time-out room, the, 61, 62
Times, having enjoyable together, 69
Timidity, 27, 53
Toilet training, 80
Tom, the case of, 209
Tone deaf, 155
Toys, how to treat the leaving of, 157
    place for storing, 95
Training to communicate, 84
Truthfulness, 8
TV, 106

-U-

Under foot, child who is always, 129
Unexpected, do the, 59
United States, 37

-V-

Value, person of, 47
Vanity, how to treat, 200, 201
Viciousness, 123
Vicissitudes, of life, 39
Voice, Your tone of, communicates too, 56

-W-

Walking, in children, 79
Walters, Richard H., 114
Watson, Goodwin, 115
Weak, the chronically, how to treat, 202, 203
Weaknesses, assumed, 203
Weaning, 104
What Do We Know About Learning, 115
What It Means to be a Mormon, by Adam S. Bennion, 17

"Wholistic" nature, of the child, 24
Withdrawal can be very effective, 64
World, provide an orderly, 96
Worthlessness, feelings of, 48

-Y-

Young, Brigham, 38
Youngest child, the characteristics of, 26
Yourself, be firm with, 65